Endorse[...]

The true visionary thinks bey[...] looks beyond into the future, many times generations ahead. Gary Klaben is that pure visionary. He helps families think, act and live multi-generational and gives them the knowledge to maximize their futures to the highest possible levels. He also is a litmus test for the people he serves as Gary always puts his own family first, living with multiple generations of Klabens with love, harmony, and pure family bonding.

—Justin Breen
Founder BrEpic Network

Gary Klaben is the real deal, the entrepreneur's entrepreneur. His *Multigenerational Living* philosophy is exactly what we need. Klaben applies successful business practices to often complex family dynamics and creates a meticulous but practical blueprint for intelligent growth and stability. He shows us the optimal structural and financial systems we need while simultaneously emphasizing the need to foster strong family bonds. That's a tall order, but Klaben does it and does it in a highly accessible way. Entrepreneurs will find this book an indispensable tool, helping them not only avoid the notorious "three-generation curse" but inspiring them to cultivate a long-lasting, prosperous, and unified family dynasty. Bravo!

—Alex Gertsburg
CEO, CoverMySix; Managing Partner,
Gertsburg Licata Law

What if there was a unique process you've probably never heard of that could help you leave something (beyond money) for future generations? Most people *never* talk about this, but families are reuniting and reinventing what's called *Multigenerational Living*, combining several generations under one roof or within one estate. Gary Klaben's new book, *Multigenerational Living*, is for busy entrepreneurs who might find it intriguing to learn more about living on a unified family estate and sharing resources across generations. As you can imagine, making it work takes careful planning. There are intricacies involved with creating a living arrangement where different generations coexist closely. With over 30 years of experience as a financial coach and with five families (four generations) living on his estate, Gary is the perfect person to guide you—and his book lays out *exactly* how to make it happen. From building a vision rooted in trust and guidelines based on your family's values to practical estate structures and step-by-step operational planning, this book can be a valuable tool for you if you want to leverage real estate to pass down lasting wealth *and* promote family closeness for generations to come.

—Joe Polish
Founder of Genius Network and Genius Recovery

Filled with practical strategies and heartfelt insights, this book is a must-read for families embracing multigenerational living. With warmth and wisdom, Gary shares valuable lessons on creating harmony and resilience within the family estate, making it an indispensable resource for anyone curious about this lifestyle.

—Gino Wickman
Author of *Traction & Shine*, Creator of EOS®

Gary Klaben's *Multigenerational Living* is not just a guide to multigenerational living; it's a strategic blueprint that rethinks traditional family structures to unlock significant value. As an entrepreneur who thrives on identifying and amplifying hidden opportunities, I found the systematic and scalable approach of this book particularly compelling. Klaben's book mirrors the business lifecycle, presenting a scalable framework that can be customized to fit any family's needs, much like my "Just Add A Zero" (JAAZ) strategy. It applies a business-minded governance model to family living while transforming conventional living setups into high-growth ventures, effectively multiplying traditional value propositions.

Multigenerational Living offers practical strategies for both wealth preservation and expansion across generations, resonating with my philosophy of transforming invisible opportunities into visible successes. Moreover, its potential to foster community resilience and sustainability illustrates the powerful ripple effects of strategic multigenerational living.

—Chad Jenkins
Author of *Just Add a Zero*

Gary Klaben's book *Multigenerational Living* offers a fresh perspective and invaluable insights for anyone considering or already engaged in multigenerational living. Blending personal experiences with professional expertise, Gary provides practical advice and actionable steps for navigating the intricacies of family estates. His emphasis on creating a lasting legacy for future generations is both inspiring and thought-provoking. Whether you're new to multigenerational living or seeking to enhance your current arrangement, this book provides indispensable guidance and encouragement for fostering harmonious family dynamics.

—Dan Sullivan
Co-Founder & President, Strategic Coach®

Gary expertly guides you through the critical steps needed to navigate this lifestyle with ease and confidence. As someone who has managed my personal multigenerational home, I understand the importance of having a reliable resource. Gary's book provides the wisdom and assurance you need to succeed. I only wish I had this invaluable guide when I started my own journey.

—Lisa M. Cini, CHID, NCIDQ, PMP
Author of *HIVE: The Simple Guide to Multigenerational Living*, Award-winning designer, Aging in Place Expert, President / CEO of Mosaic Design Studio

MULTIGENERATIONAL LIVING

The Proven Guide to Creating Stronger Families and Smarter Finances through Intentionally Designed Shared Spaces

Other Books by Gary Klaben

*Changing the Conversation:
Transformational Steps to Financial and Family Well-Being*

Wealth of Everything

The Business Battlefield
(co-authored with Adam Blonsky)

MULTIGENERATIONAL LIVING

The Proven Guide to Creating Stronger Families and Smarter Finances through Intentionally Designed Shared Spaces

GARY KLABEN

ethos
collective

MULTIGENERATIONAL LIVING © 2024 by Gary Klaben.
All rights reserved.

Printed in the United States of America

Published by Ethos Collective™
PO Box 43, Powell, OH 43065
EthosCollective.vip

This book contains material protected under international and federal copyright laws and treaties. Any unauthorized reprint or use of this material is prohibited. No part of this book may be reproduced or transmitted in any form or by any means, electronic or mechanical, including photocopying, recording, or by any information storage and retrieval system, without express written permission from the author.

LCCN: 2024906580
Paperback ISBN: 978-1-63680-274-9
Hardcover ISBN: 978-1-63680-275-6
e-book ISBN: 978-1-63680-276-3

Available in paperback, hardcover, e-book, and audiobook.

Any Internet addresses (websites, blogs, etc.) and telephone numbers printed in this book are offered as a resource. They are not intended in any way to be or imply an endorsement by Ethos Collective™, nor does Ethos Collective™ vouch for the content of these sites and numbers for the life of this book.

Some names and identifying details may have been changed to protect the privacy of individuals.

DEDICATION

To the seven generations and over 110 souls, from my great-grandparents who taught me to play Pinochle to my great-grandniece who is learning to walk and talk.

Table of Contents

Foreword xiii
Introduction xvii

Chapter 1:   The First Step 1
Chapter 2:   What Is a Normal Family Living
             Arrangement? 7

Stage One: Foundational Development

Chapter 3:   Wealth Management Today 17
Chapter 4:   Trust and Communication 21
Chapter 5:   Conflict Resolution 27
Chapter 6:   Vision. 32
Chapter 7:   Governance 38

Stage Two: Structure

Chapter 8:   Structure 47
Chapter 9:   From Discernment to Consensus 51

Chapter 10: Process of Elimination 57
Chapter 11: Financial Stress Test 64
Chapter 12: The Estate Structure 71
Chapter 13: Timeline and Selection Criteria 77

Stage Three: The Multigenerational Living Estate Transaction

Chapter 14: Setting Expectations................ 85
Chapter 15: Location......................... 89
Chapter 16: Search Parameters 94
Chapter 17: Overchoice...................... 100
Chapter 18: The Contract 105
Chapter 19: Multigenerational Living Estate
             Transaction Meetings.............. 111

Stage Four: The Estate Transformation

Chapter 20: Day One, A Learning, or Winning,
             Mindset 119
Chapter 21: Multigenerational Living Estate Visits . 125
Chapter 22: The Multigenerational Living Estate
             Operating Platform 130
Chapter 23: Financials, Business, and Philanthropy. . 137
Chapter 24: Family Security................... 144
Chapter 25: Daily and Seasonal Fun and
             Family Traditions 148

Conclusion..................................... 153
Endnotes 157
Acknowledgments 159
About the Author................................ 161

Foreword

I love Coretta Scott King's quote, "The greatness of a community is most accurately measured by the compassionate actions of its members," because it resembles the very essence of Gary Klaben. He is an "Others First" leader. For over a decade, I have had the opportunity to know, work with, and experience Gary Klaben's wisdom and generosity as he works with others. He is a true leader who leans on his faith to lead for the benefit of others.

It is a privilege to introduce Gary's insightful book, *Multigenerational Living*. This work resonates deeply with the enduring values that many of us hold dear, where the focus is on the flow of resources, relationships, and responsibilities across generations rather than the accumulation of wealth in isolation.

In a world increasingly characterized by volatility, uncertainty, complexity, and ambiguity (VUCA), the principles of multigenerational living offer a stable and enriching alternative. Gary Klaben masterfully addresses the challenges and opportunities of bringing multiple generations under one roof, creating a living arrangement that emphasizes trust, communication, and a shared vision for the future. His approach to multigenerational estates, built on a foundation of mutual respect and shared values, is a blueprint for families aspiring to thrive together, fostering enduring wealth that transcends monetary value.

Multigenerational Living is a vital resource for entrepreneurs and families who seek to build a legacy that endures through generations. It challenges the traditional notion of wealth transfer and offers a more holistic and sustainable approach. Gary's vision of multigenerational living is more than just a practical guide; it is an invitation to reimagine how we live, work, and grow together as families. By focusing on clear communication, conflict resolution, and the establishment of a shared family vision, he provides the tools necessary to create harmonious and sustainable family estates.

Gary's insights into the importance of a shared family vision, trust-building, and conflict resolution are crucial elements for any family considering multigenerational living. He offers practical advice on setting expectations, defining roles, and creating governance structures that ensure the smooth operation and long-term success of multigenerational estates. These steps are essential in avoiding the common pitfalls of wealth transfer, where many families fail to sustain their wealth beyond the third generation.

Moreover, *Multigenerational Living* emphasizes the significance of a strong family foundation built on shared values and principles. Gary's experiences and lessons learned from his own journey into multigenerational living provide invaluable guidance for families embarking on this path. His approach highlights the importance of preparing future generations to manage and grow the wealth they inherit, ensuring that it contributes positively to their lives and the lives of those around them.

Multigenerational Living

This book also touches on the broader societal implications of multigenerational living, suggesting that it can help address some of the pressing issues of our time, such as housing affordability, social isolation, and the need for sustainable living practices. By bringing families together, we can create more resilient and supportive communities that thrive on mutual aid and cooperation.

Multigenerational Living is not just a manual for creating a multigenerational home; it is a call to action for families to think deeply about their legacy and the values they want to pass on to future generations. It encourages us to look beyond the immediate benefits of financial wealth and consider the enduring impact of our choices on the lives of our descendants.

I invite you to delve into *Multigenerational Living* with an open heart and mind, ready to embrace the principles that will not only enhance your family's financial well-being but also its emotional, spiritual, and relational wealth. Let us embark on this journey of creating multigenerational living spaces that are not just houses but homes filled with love, purpose, and enduring wealth.

—Lee Brower
Founder of Empowered Wealth, Author,
International Speaker, and Gratitude Advocate

Introduction

A new trend has exploded in recent years–work from home. But alongside this trend is another you might not have heard of yet. We're seeing a new internal migration happening in the United States: families are again reuniting and reinventing the trend of multigenerational living—combining several generations under one roof or within one estate.

Most people are familiar with a nuclear family. It consists of parents and their children living in a single-family residence. This living model was born out of necessity when young people and families moved to the cities for employment. The industrialization of farming eliminated their livelihood, while the small businesses born out of the Industrial Revolution beckoned.

Growing up, my nuclear family consisted of twelve people: my nine siblings, along with mom and dad. I loved growing up in our large family and believe there is no better way to live. Family and everything related to the health, well-being, and happiness of family members is always at the forefront of my mind. It has become my agenda for my family and all the families I support in my professional career. I was able to identify this as my primary purpose in life at an early age. My purpose, my "why," is always being fascinated and motivated to help each person I meet on how to think about and make smart decisions with their money. For most of my life, I've helped families, multi-generationally, to live fully, grow their wealth, and then successfully pass it on to the next generation.

My career in wealth management started like many other professionals. The typical delivery of investment management services, along with helping clients with their other wealth issues, extended out of investment management. There was no pursuit of a deeper dive beyond their money as it extended to their family.

And then, one day, it happened. Everything changed.

It was a beautiful summer morning on a Saturday in 1991. We were meeting with our clients, Pete and Gail, along with their attorney, to sign their newly drafted estate documents. I was looking forward to meeting their two adult children, whom they had spoken about many times. Their children could only make a Saturday meeting due to work commitments to sign their respective documents as they related to their parents' estate.

The attorney reviewed each document, followed by them being witnessed, signed and notarized. A well-executed plan was now in place to service the next two generations. A job well done . . . or at least I thought so.

After saying our goodbyes and heading home, I began to have this bad sinking feeling—you know, a bad deep-down feeling alerting me that something was just not right. I thought of my family—Deb and our children—they were fine—nothing there. My extended family, my friends, my colleagues—nothing there. And then it struck me!

It was like a thunderbolt of fear and anxiety. It felt like I had been a party to a crime. Not a crime of the present

Multigenerational Living

but one that would play out over the lifetimes of Pete and Gail's family.

I had just met their two adult children. They were neophytes when it came to money. Sure, they knew how to make money and pay bills, but they had no clue how to deal with millions of dollars of inheritance. You see, we had just executed documents that immediately saved Pete and Gail around $2 million in estate taxes. Based on these newly signed documents, each child would receive an additional million dollars.

Not only would their children receive the large inheritance in place before signing the documents, but they now will receive even more money. I had just been involved in adding more fuel to the fire. The fire of money dominated soul-sucking slaves to the almighty dollar. Not good. I could feel the blood draining from my face. I had to do everything possible not to turn my car around and go back to the office to tear up and burn the newly signed documents. It was that powerful of a deep, visceral jolt to my being.

I had a choice. Do I continue to help my clients solve their money and estate issues regardless of the outcome for their future generations, or do I proactively do something about it?

As you may have guessed, I decided to begin the process of working with the second and third generations to prepare them for the wealth they will receive. I wanted to make certain they would, like their parents, be good stewards of their money—master their money, not become addicted to it, slaves to it.

Even though it takes time—5, 10, or 20 years—I will not be a part of any family that does not address their future generation's relationship to money.

This drives me each day. It is why I exist. It is why this book has been written. The remainder of this book provides the unvarnished truth of living multi-generationally. At times, you may be wondering why you would ever consider this new lifestyle after reading many of these chapters. Place those chapters in context. They are written to provide you with the full truth of living this lifestyle. They do not define this lifestyle.

I absolutely, positively love living with the five families on our estate! Everyone is a work in progress. We are all just trying to live our lives out to fulfill what we feel is why we are here on Earth. The support, the joy, the camaraderie, and the fun are here all the time.

Before we dive into how to create successful multi-generational living, it's important to understand how to achieve success. Americans define success as creating a legacy by leaving their wealth primarily to loved ones who are properly prepared to accept it and have the wisdom to grow and thrive with their newfound wealth. However, passing on wealth from generation to generation has historically had dismal results in the United States. Studies confirm that over 91 percent of families completely fail to maintain the wealth passed on to them after the third generation. They are simply not prepared for this "sudden wealth." The family goes from shirtsleeves to shirtsleeves in three generations. This is also true in Eastern culture, defined as rice paddies to rice paddies in three generations. How, or even more so, why does this happen?

The first-generation wealth builders typically leave the money without an "instruction manual" on how to spend, save, invest, or manage wealth. Ultimately, an unhealthy relationship and dependence on money develops that affects the future generations on emotional, physical, and spiritual levels, leaving the third generation without the knowledge and ability to manage the wealth. This is unacceptable to me and why I'm adamant about helping

Multigenerational Living

families make sure their future generations are better prepared to operate with the wealth they receive.

Coaching my clients about their money and passing it on to the next generation strikes home with me on a personal level. In 2016, our family established a goal—a vision statement narrative—to purchase a second home where our family could gather and enjoy one another during the summer months. In a later chapter, you will learn a different, more effective, and timely approach to coming up with a family vision narrative. Had we applied what we now know back then, we would have saved our family a lot of time, money, and energy.

After a few years and many discussions, we decided to buy a full-time property for two families, ours and our daughter's, for our three generations to live multi-generationally. As life progressed through its twists and turns, closely related families joined us. We now have five families living on our estate (four generations). Through the process of trial and error, we've learned a lot about how this whole process works. Before long, people in our network started to ask how they could start their own multigenerational living. It became apparent that this trend, accelerated by COVID-19, the rising costs of living, and the ability to work remotely, is picking up speed.

This book is written for the busy, successful entrepreneur who wants to consider multigenerational living on an estate. It serves as a practical guide and explores how to create a living arrangement where different generations coexist closely, providing insights and advice on understanding and navigating the intricacies of multigenerational living. Whether it's a family ranch, cottage, sprawling family compound, estate, or any name that resonates with the unique identity of the place where you and your related family dwell, this book is your companion in navigating the nuances of multigenerational living.

This book will walk you through the whys and hows to set up, establish, and grow while living multi-generationally. The following pages will uncover the truths and myths behind this style of living, along with the successes and failures we've experienced along the way. Living multi-generationally is a fundamental lifestyle shift from the independent, nuclear family living arrangement. Let's explore it together.

1
The First Step

Before you can jump into living multi-generationally, someone has to intentionally decide to consider starting on a new path in life. That person sees a future much bigger than the past. Who in your family will take the first step on your journey to multigenerational living?

Simon Sinek did a TEDx Talk in 2014 titled "How Great Leaders Inspire Action," which, as of this writing, has been viewed over sixty million times. The short version of his talk explains to start with "why." Why do you want to begin this journey toward multigenerational living? Simply stated, what is the meaning and purpose behind your vision of your future? That's right. This is about being the visionary and taking the first step to express your vision to your family. And because you are reading this book, the "why" starts with you.

Some people never really figure out their why. They spend their entire life trying to determine what they do when they grow up (their "why"). The vision narrative stems from the "why." You cannot gloss over or skip this step if you want your vision to be successful.

Once you have your "why," it's time to consider how to communicate your vision of the future of living multi-generationally on your estate. Before we get to the technique to do this, one that I've used for decades in my coaching, we'll review two important concepts: pushing yourself forward and pulling yourself forward. These are two very different ways you can move forward, and one is more effective than the other.

Pushing Yourself Forward

Most people choose the pushing forward method. For example, imagine your goal is to establish a multigenerational living estate in precisely three years with your parents and your sibling's family on at least twenty acres with fields, forest, and a stream within a one-hour drive of Denver, Colorado. That was the goal. Fairly straightforward. It is written in the typical goal format you've seen put forth by most self-help books, personal coaches, and mentors. But is this method of goal-setting the most effective way to achieve what you want? Does it make your goals tangible?

Pull Yourself Forward

Alternatively, you can pull yourself to the future you envision. Where do you picture yourself in the future, both mentally and spiritually? Then, describe, in great detail, what your vision looks like from that future. Write your vision in the present tense. Write as if the goal, your vision, has been achieved. Be exact and specific about describing every important aspect of what your vision of that future looks, feels, and is, in our example, three years from today.

This leads to the second concept: making your future normal. Dan Sullivan, the co-founder with Babs Smith of Strategic Coach®, describes a concept he terms the Here/

Multigenerational Living

There Model™. For our purposes, "Here" is where you are right now. "There" happens three years from now, living multi-generationally on your estate.

Dan expresses a very important principle with the Here/There Model. To make something normal, we must be present in the There. Instead of speaking about the future as a place we are going to, we instead speak about it in the present. Making something normal to yourself allows you and others involved in this new normal to get comfortable with this future normal being present today.

The magic is making the vision of a bigger future for your family absolutely normal to you. When we normalize something, we place ourselves in that environment as if it has already happened. Normalizing my vision of the future sets up my mindset. My brain then tirelessly and continuously seeks out and attracts everything and everyone necessary to make this vision come true.

This approach pulls you toward the future you want. Pulling is ten times more powerful than pushing. Pulling is like a vortex continuously seeking out people, resources, money, knowledge, learning, and everything else necessary for you and your family to achieve the multigenerational future you have envisioned.

Pulling Forward Exercise

To begin pulling toward your future, put on your make-believe hat. Place yourself into the future you seek. Write about your vision, backed by your purpose and meaning (your "why"), in the present tense. Don't hesitate. Play along with me. (This is powerful!)

Imagine boarding a helicopter that takes you to the top of the mountain you seek to climb—your multigenerational living estate. You step off the helicopter and look down the mountain to the place you are right now, the present. From your perch on top of the mountain, you can view the easiest path with the fewest obstacles, switchbacks, and dangerous trail headings to reach the mountain top easily.

Write down the vision of multigenerational living on your estate in as much detail as possible. It may be something like this.

> It's three years from today, _/_/_. My parents, my sister's family, and my family are living multi-generationally on our estate. We now live on forty acres with a pond, two streams, and ten acres of tillable fields, along with thirty acres of pristine Colorado mixed evergreen forest. We are five hundred feet in elevation above Denver, a forty-five-minute drive from our new home. There are top-notch hospitals within thirty minutes. The airport is a one-hour drive, providing easy access for periodic business trips along with other travel.
>
> The school district is top-rated, with middle and high schools within a ten-minute drive. My sister's and our children will be attending these schools and are building relationships with other families like ours in the area. All major shopping is within a twenty-minute drive, providing the convenience we desire to keep life as easy and simple as possible. We have eliminated noise and air pollution. It's dark and quiet at night, allowing us to have complete restful sleep, thereby allowing us to start each day off refreshed and eager to meet the day.
>
> We used to live in a suburb of Denver to make the short ten-minute daily commute to work. After COVID-19, we are no longer required to be in the office every day. In fact, my schedule allows me to drive into the office once or twice weekly. My sister and her husband lived in Chicago. They both have jobs that are primarily remote. Once a month, they need to travel to Chicago for business meetings.

Multigenerational Living

> The property is awesome! We have three separate homes that are one-minute walking distance apart. There is a fourth building with kitchen facilities allowing us to gather as a family for celebrations, break bread together, or simply be with each other. One big advantage is we've formed an LLC and Homeowners Association to buy the property and share expenses. Without this arrangement, we would not have been able to purchase and maintain this property.
>
> Early on, we held meetings and went through a formal process of clear communication to establish a stronger, trusting relationship between our families. We discussed and practiced conflict resolution exercises to get comfortable with uncomfortable situations that will eventually show up in the future.

After each adult family member provided their own vision of their future, we revised the original vision statement. Ultimately, what you see above is an example of what will come out of the work you do to come up with a common written vision statement.

There is more about this process that we will discuss as the book progresses, but you get the idea. The more you flesh out the future you envision for yourself and your family, the easier it is to make it normal. More importantly, this exercise allows you and your family to be propelled to the future you envision. This first step of visioning gives you a strong foundation. You have been intentional and exact about what your future looks like. Your subconscious brain is now working behind the scenes, actively seeking out everything and anything that will make the future you envisioned come to fruition.

Nothing worthwhile moves forward until we first sell ourselves and become clear about where we are going. You have taken the first step and sold yourself on this vision. This journey toward multigenerational living on an estate started with you. Now, communicate your vision to one or more other close family members—the ones who may want to join you on this journey.

2

What Is a Normal Family Living Arrangement?

Before we delve into talking about who will join you on this multigenerational journey, let's examine how families live. Every society, culture, people, or nationality has formally or informally agreed upon norms. Humans like to understand and comply with what "normal" is in every facet of human living. Young children, being inquisitive and curious, question everything. We find ourselves explaining why someone or something is normal. As society changes over time, we begin to accept new norms. Today, we see half a dozen different types of normal family arrangements: nuclear families, extended families, single-parent, blended or reconstituted families, same-sex families, and childless families.

What's Old Is New Again

We have become familiar and comfortable with the norm of a nuclear family. And whatever is normal becomes part of our belief system. When we are introduced to a possible new normal, it clashes with our current belief system. We won't readily change what we believe to be true overnight. It takes time to adjust to the new. Multigenerational living seems archaic and even culturally out of touch with normal society. It's as if the multigenerational family hasn't learned how to live in modern society. Some may believe it borders on being a cult. Your vision of multigenerational living on an estate is a foreign concept that may clash with your closest family members' belief system. It will most likely take time for your vision of the future to sink in and be accepted as a possible new normal.

Centuries ago, hunter/gatherer societies turned into agrarian societies. Eventually, feudal societies formed and then gave way to the early Industrial Revolution and the emergence of the nuclear family. This transition from an agrarian to feudal society to industrial capitalist systems in the eighteenth and nineteenth centuries is one of the primary reasons for this historical shift. Before the Industrial Revolution, extended families often lived together in farming communities, sharing labor and resources. However, with industrialization came urbanization, as many people moved to cities seeking employment. This migration broke up the extended family unit and introduced the nuclear family, which required much less living space.

A nuclear family is defined as parents and their children. We have lived with and been surrounded by other nuclear families in our suburban and urban environments. Eventually, children grow up, leave, and start their own nuclear families in the same geographical location. Or, those grown children may accept a job opportunity in a distant location away from their original nuclear family.

Parents live through the painful process of having to be separated from their children as they go off into the world, first for education, then for a job, and finally, through

Multigenerational Living

marriage into another family. Many parents and children count the days when they can reconnect with each other. If and when grandchildren are born, the pull to be together grows stronger. Such is the lifestyle of the majority of Americans.

In the United States, it's typical to think of multigenerational living as a family living on family farms with two or three homes co-located in close proximity to the main barn and other agricultural facilities. In this narrative, grandma and grandpa originally took over the land from a parent, raised their family in the larger house, then moved to a smaller one while one of their children moved into the big house with their family and continued farming operations. Grandma and grandpa may still help out with chores to relieve some of the pressure on their child of raising a family while operating a full-time farming venture.

With this stereotype at the forefront of many people's minds, you may experience your family members asking themselves how applicable and appropriate it is to consider reforming your family's lifestyle into a multigenerational one. However, many people have entertained the possibility of living close to or with a close family member, especially during the summer of 2020 when being disconnected was the norm, and we were all wondering how long this "temporary" condition would persist.

With the introduction of COVID-19 in 2020, the trend toward multigenerational living gained momentum. Children living in cramped quarters in the city moved back in with their parents to be connected at a time when everything was about social distancing and isolation everywhere. With modern societies' changing dynamics, the multigenerational living style is gaining newfound attention and relevance.

Adopting a New Lifestyle

You may be eager to take this step, nevertheless, moving near to and cohabitating with your close family members is a life-changing decision. Who do you initially share your vision with? Do you share it with a close family member who may give you a realistic response to the impact your vision will have on other family members who may want to join you on this multigenerational living adventure? This is the moment of truth. Your family members may react differently when they realize what following through with your "crazy" idea will entail. Your other initiatives did not involve them personally—they could watch your successes and your failures safely from a distance. Not so with this idea.

No one is excited about being a part of someone else's failed idea. Failing on our own ideas is not pleasant, but we accept that possibility. We judge ourselves by our intentions—we judge others by their actions. You are battling their perception of reality because, to them, your vision seems like wishful thinking. Although your vision narrative will help illustrate the completely fleshed-out thinking behind your purpose for living multi-generationally, they will need time to fully absorb, understand, and accept it as a possible new reality.

If your family has already fully embraced the notion of living multi-generationally, your detailed vision of the future may be welcomed more openly. Your family members will begin to entertain the efficacy of the various aspects of your vision narrative.

Although it's easy to communicate via phone and e-mail these days, presenting the vision narrative to your family members needs to be done in person. If you are accustomed to having family meetings, then it's only a matter of scheduling a family meeting. Certainly, a time

Multigenerational Living

and place conducive to sharing your vision of living multi-generationally must be carefully selected. Your family may be ready to go. They may have been waiting for you to go through your "journey to the mountain" to gather your thoughts and contemplate your version of multigenerational living on an estate.

But what if your family is not ready to go? You may be met with opposition, concern, frustration, anxiety, or other negative responses. How do you address and appropriately communicate the essence of your grand vision and purpose? You certainly believe it matches some deep-down purpose they may have to live multi-generationally, but in this case, you'll need to spend time communicating your vision thoroughly as well as an idea of what their family vision could be.

Recently, I interviewed twenty families who have established multi-generational households from one hundred years ago through today. Some of them are going through the process of starting their multigenerational living in the next few years. There are so many lessons to learn from those who formed their situations many years ago.

One successful wealthy entrepreneur wanted to build a multigenerational living estate on five thousand acres he purchased in Montana. He spent over $8 million on homes and facilities to house four families, his and the families of his three children. After three years of construction and build-out, it was time for everyone to move in.

But no one moved in. This gentleman did not communicate or receive feedback about whether his family, including his wife, wanted to move to Montana and live multi-generationally. His

approach in business, as a successful entrepreneur, did not translate into that same success on the home front. His focus and purpose was on what he believed his family wanted. Years later, after selling the property, he realized he had not truly listened to what his family wanted. They had repeatedly let him know they would not move to this property for a multitude of reasons. He never seriously considered any of those reasons.

Building a Strong Foundation

Visionaries, although listened to, followed, and accepted, have a bad track record, according to most outside observers. Many of you have arrows in your back from being the first to venture into uncharted territory. While your family's purpose may align with yours in considering the next most important step of multigenerational living, your ability to clearly express your vision of the future and lead your family along this new path is not a given.

Wanting to be part of the 9 percent of successful families who avoided going from shirtsleeves to shirtsleeves in three generations requires a very strong foundational starting point. The first stage in establishing multigenerational living on your family estate is to go through the necessary foundational work required to achieve the highest degree of success. To do this, you must cover several important arenas.

1. **Establish trust:** This is accomplished through clear and open communication.
2. **Conflict resolution:** It's important to understand and practice how to deal with differences. (Establishing trust first helps with this step.) Conflict resolution

Multigenerational Living

will be critical throughout your multigenerational living experience.

3. **Vision statement:** Once steps one and two have been completed, you can develop the vision statement for the whole family. To do this, each adult family member puts together and shares their vision of multigenerational living on one estate. One person will be responsible for merging all the statements, and every adult member will need to agree on the vision statement.

4. **Rules, boundaries, procedures, and SOPs:** This is established through a formal governance document signed by all family members, whether or not they participate in living multi-generationally on the estate. Multigenerational living is not inclusive of those family members living in close proximity on the estate. Those other family members who chose not to live on the estate or are not able to due to family or work related reasons have a say and part in the governance of the family.

5. **Family Council:** Establish a family council composed of the leadership of the family during the process of setting up the system of governance. You may decide to have a separate "estate" council that reports to the family council. They will manage all the moving parts that require outside help and assistance just to maintain and address issues that arise daily.

* * *

Before you dive into the financial aspects of selecting a property, you must develop a strong Foundation.

STAGE ONE
Foundational Development

3

Wealth Management Today

For more than thirty years, I've been a part of the wealth management world. There have been accepted norms for establishing and growing a successful wealth management business. Working with extended family members and leaving wealth in capable hands are generally considered afterthoughts to the primary focus of investment management. (In some circles, working with these family members is a complete no-no!)

No wonder we see the abysmal history of shirtsleeves to shirtsleeves in three generations. The wealth management industry shies away from anything that is not highly profitable, and addressing the future generations and their needs is unprofitable. The industry teaches advisors to invest assets and offer new products and services as laws change and clients go through predictable stages of life. But, under no circumstances are advisers to conduct business or provide services to non-paying family members. Doing so will certainly diminish profit margin and open up Pandora's Box of never-ending non-paid work.

The agenda is to engage with a new client by addressing their money wants, needs, and concerns. Once that is completed, they move on to the estate-planning issues. The estate planning is handed off to a law firm to complete the necessary documents. There is little follow-up because there is no money in it for the adviser. Yet, over the many years I've worked with clients, invariably, the first question I'm asked after handling their money, their "investable assets," is, "Can you help my children?"

This question is a natural response after getting your money in order: turning your attention to your children. Why? Every parent wants their children and their grandchildren to be better off than them. Parents want their heirs to master their wealth with confidence, clarity, and comfort, so they make smart decisions with their newfound wealth, even with those children who may be estranged from their parents. This makes sense. First, take care of your money and wealth, then address the transfer of your values and core tenets around money to your children. Traditionally, only the mechanical transfer of wealth is addressed.

Those few wealth managers who understand this fundamental need make it a priority to address their client's estate plan in coordination and discussion with their estate planning attorney, accountant, and other necessary professionals. But this is far from the norm.

A New Focus for Building Wealth

The commonly accepted formulaic approach does not work when establishing multigenerational living. Everything is backward. Establishing a multigenerational living estate changes the center of gravity from the initial wealth builders to the family. This flies in the face of the common perception of how to establish, build, and grow wealth.

Multigenerational Living

When building wealth through business endeavors, the entrepreneur's focus is narrowly defined. The focus personally is on you and your nuclear family's needs supported by the business enterprise as the children are growing up.

First-generation wealth builders vigorously pursue estate planning in an isolated environment. I compare this to the "big gender reveal" parties about a future newborn child. That big reveal, when proactively pursued, happens during the lifetime of the first generation. The unknown and perceived scary Money Monster is that the second generation will sit back on their laurels as soon as they discover the great amount of wealth they will receive, taking on a ne'er-do-well approach until Dad and Mom pass.

One truly can't be certain of the response by second generation family members. In my experience, parents are fairly astute in recognizing the effect of drawing back the curtain to reveal their estate's value and what effect it will have on their future generations. Some families leave their wealth in the hands of professional trustees who dole out the money to meet living expenses, while the future generations have a poor relationship with money or a history of financial abuse.

When establishing multigenerational living on an estate, the focus shifts to a common vision/purpose agreed upon by those who want to live multi-generationally. Does it align perfectly? Of course not. There is discernment followed by consensus, resulting in an agreed-upon joint vision with the appropriate agreed-upon governance.

Wealth Dispersal

Families who proactively plan out their estate and communicate how it will be dispersed upon their death can still do this when establishing a multigenerational living estate. Generally, this is considered after the "living" estate is properly structured, invested, and monitored. Addressing the estate distribution takes second place after making certain there is the necessary cash flow to successfully live multi-generationally on the estate.

The estate's vision/purpose and future of the estate is addressed first. This is when the issue of how the money will be structured, invested, and distributed comes up. If family members don't want to live multi-generationally within the structure, governance, and envisioned lifestyle, now is the time to find out.

The money discussion is a whole different issue requiring the development of a financial stress test to determine what parameters need to be surfaced and addressed. Some families begin with the primary support of the first-generation wealth builders' cash flow and assets. Other families combine their finances to make multi-generational living a financial success. The money side of multigenerational living will be covered in greater detail at the end of the next stage. (See Chapter 11.) You can see the importance of having open and truthful conversations with all family members when discussing all matters, including finances.

* * *

The following chapter explores how you can build communication and trust between and among your family members, allowing everyone to be fully heard and understood.

4

Trust and Communication

Many years ago, while serving in the United States Army, I found myself sharing very few interests with some of the enlisted soldiers under my charge. As an officer, I had a duty to care for my soldiers, placing their needs above my own. The quandary was how to effectively serve someone I had nothing in common with. Unfortunately, it wasn't until a few years later, through discussions with my spiritual mentor, that I discovered how to think about and address others who are much different from myself.

Every human being on the planet, all eight billion of us, has two things in common: we all deserve dignity and respect from every other person. Dignity and respect turn out to be a solid way to start any relationship, and continued effective communication establishes and builds trust.

The Basics of Communication

Before we get into the intricacies of communication and trust in a multigenerational environment, it's important to understand how complex this is. In a nuclear family, we interact and communicate with fewer people. Rules and boundaries are simpler and easier to observe and implement. Communication and trust are necessary and easier to establish. Life is easier with fewer family members.

Many years ago, studies were conducted on primates to determine how many could effectively live together. Researchers noticed that happy, successful primate groups generally numbered 15–18. With eighteen primates, there are a total of 153 relationships for each primate to observe, communicate with, and understand. These 153 relationships were the cognitive limit of primates to live within the social norms of other related primates.

The evolutionary psychologist Robin Dunbar studied the number of individuals a human can maintain a stable social relationship with and be capable of knowing who each member is and how they relate to every other person. That number is 150 (Dunbar's number).[1] That means we can keep track of an astounding 11,175 different relationships!

Let's pare down that number and consider a nuclear family of four individuals. There are only six total relationships to recognize, understand, and communicate with effectively. Putting three, four-person nuclear families together equals twelve individuals. There are now sixty-six relationships to understand and communicate effectively with. That is over a tenfold increase! Some family members are bound to not get along well with a few of the other family members in such an extended family living environment.

Trust and communication are the critical factors in the families we interviewed who have long-term established multigenerational living situations. One family leader noted their attitude is one where each person has the other's best interest at heart. Another noted that every family is expected to take care of their own. A third stated, "There is an urgency, an underlying vibration to do what's best." These family leaders understand that the critical importance and necessity of this first stage is to build a solid foundation of mutual trust and clear communication.

Clear, simple, and effective communication, along with building trust, determines the future success of cohabitation on an estate. This stage must not be skipped!

Building Trust

Spending time discussing, discerning, and understanding how others want to be listened to and understood is critical. When a conflict arises, how is it to be handled and rectified? Will the strong bond of trust be nurtured or degraded?

One successful example of this is taken from an interview we conducted. Deep multigenerational trust and communication contributed to one family's success by maintaining a very strong bond between twenty-two cousins representing two major branches of the family. Their ability to communicate and trust each other is a core foundational aspect of this family being able to build and maintain a legacy that has now, after almost one hundred years, reached into the sixth generation.

Lack of communication and trust is one of the key reasons why 91 percent of wealthy families do not survive beyond three generations. In *Preparing Heirs*, Roy Williams and Vic Preisser relate that 60 percent of families failed primarily due to a lack of communication and trust.[2] That is a startling statistic. Imagine how many of them would have survived beyond three generations if the majority of families had established strong, trusted relationships with clear and appropriate communication.

Many popular diagnostic tools, such as DISC®, Thomas-Kilmann Conflict Instrument®, or the Stratton Interpersonal Leadership Style survey, address and identify an individual's leadership and communication style. As we all know, family members can blend like oil and water and never understand one another. However, once they recognize each other's communication style, they may respond to it and grow to respect the other person's communicative approach. This will lead to the long-lasting, strong, and trusted relationships necessary for multigenerational living.

Communication

We don't trust others we don't understand. Every day, we see this play out in large and small organizations. Fortunately for us, those outside organizations are not permanent fixtures in our lives; we can remove ourselves from them. But this is not easily done with family.

You've seen advice such as "A private life is a happy life" or "Keep your business to yourself." With a nuclear family, not addressing these communication issues with those we don't interact with daily is not as pressing due to time and distance. Once children go out into the world and build their own nuclear family, one generation may not deal with one or more members of future generations on a daily basis. Perhaps you've heard or even said to others, "Not to worry. The holidays will be over soon, and everyone will go home."

Contrast this to a multigenerational living situation. Living multi-generationally means being in closer contact more often with other family members whom you may not get along with easily. Open and clear communication is key to maintaining trust, and trust is foundational to all relationships. However, open communication can't occur

Multigenerational Living

without trust—they are codependent. As soon as we lose trust in another person, communication becomes difficult. Every interaction is called into question. When we trust another person, we feel safe and confident they will not hurt or violate that trust. We can be vulnerable and open up without becoming defensive to protect ourselves.

So, how do we nurture the communication-trust relationship?

Personal and Family Values

Our identity is intertwined with our values. Like a fingerprint, they are the part of our identity that makes us unique. Sharing our personal values with other family members helps them to understand what we identify with and how our motivation and behavior show up in our daily lives. It is a cornerstone of open communication.

Hearing, seeing, and understanding other family members' values goes a long way to improving communication among family members. We fear what we don't know or don't understand. Sometimes, just one value fact can make all the difference. It is those little things (in your mind's eye) that make the difference in your relationship with someone else. Over time, we learn this with those who are close to us. For those we don't know well, we must continue our efforts to learn their communication style and work towards understanding them. The payoff will be a stronger familial bond with those individuals.

Personal values, along with shared family values, are critical to form a family values-based statement. The statement is who you are as a family. (We will develop this statement more in Chapter 6.) Once each family member discovers their values and learns the value of others, you can establish a deeper sharing and understanding around the core values of the family.

Select one of the diagnostic tools mentioned in the Building Trust section and take your family through an exercise to identify communication styles and preferences. Determine the values each person identifies with, which will provide the foundation for the next step: dealing with conflict resolution.

In the next chapter, we'll look at how to communicate effectively with each other when conflicts arise. Understanding how to successfully manage conflict resolution will help keep the family together and maintain the trust to live harmoniously as a multigenerational family for many generations to come.

5

Conflict Resolution

Entrepreneurs have a different mindset than other family members living on the estate, which is why it is important they understand W. Edwards Deming's 85/15 rule when forming a multigenerational living estate. The rule states that 85 percent of faults lie with systems, processes, structures, and practices in an organization, and only 15 percent are people-related.[3]

Entrepreneurs, when they are first-generation wealth builders, have an innovative mindset and are accustomed to overcoming obstacles by any lawful means possible to successfully build a business. They develop skills that allow them to accomplish difficult tasks and persevere through difficult times. Most of these skills are inward-facing. Entrepreneurs depend primarily on their gut feelings, instincts, and their willingness to change along with developing mastery of the required skills in their chosen field. This mindset and approach are ineffective when successfully building a multigenerational estate. That statement seems counterintuitive. It is. Entrepreneurs, as we are fond of noting, are unhirable. Let me explain.

My experience coaching and advising entrepreneurs over the past four decades has revealed their inability to effectively lead long-term multigenerational organizations or families. Simply put, they become bored and impatient and move on to the next shiny object. They like to imagine an idea and maybe make it real, but not make it repeatable. Multigenerational living on an estate is about making everything smooth, easy, and repeatable.

You May Not Be the Leader

Most of the time, we entrepreneurs enjoy tuning into our favorite radio station (WIIFM) or What's In It for ME. It's in our nature to do so. This inward-looking mindset, although natural to us, is not effective in helping us resolve conflicts when they arise.

The multigenerational estate needs the entrepreneur's vision to get things started. But just like Moses leading the Israelites out of Egypt, the entrepreneur-minded visionary doesn't have the skills to lead us to the Promised Land. Most entrepreneurs address conflict resolution somewhat in the same way they do other obstacles: They figure out how to go through it, around it, over it, or just flat-out avoid it. This works in the fast-paced, no-holds-barred entrepreneurial world but fails miserably when forming and growing a multigenerational living estate. Family members are more likely to force the entrepreneur to leave than they are to leave the estate.

One of the families I interviewed found out the hard way. Four family branches lived on this family farm. One of the fourth-generation family members married and moved on to the farm with her husband. That's when the difficulty began.

Apparently, this husband was causing a lot of commotion through late-night and early-morning activities involving inappropriate parties, illegal hunting, and, in general, disturbing the peace. Almost on a daily basis.

The other three family third-generation leadership members decided he had to leave the family farm and proceeded to "evict" him. His in-laws (a fourth-family branch) were enraged and forced a sale of the property, thereby disbanding all the families to move to individual new locations and disuniting four family branches. Their multigenerational living situation, more of a family farm with ancillary business, was sold off ninety years after surviving five generations.

How could one individual create such a disruption? In this case, the families didn't have a formal governance agreement to discipline unruly family members. Such a document could have saved this long-term multigenerational family. Governance will be covered in an upcoming chapter, but this is a cautionary tale of what can happen when our mindset is primarily inward-looking and we don't have a means for conflict resolution.

Establish a Family-Oriented Focus

Setting up a multigenerational estate is not an entrepreneurial endeavor, although it can be under the right circumstances. With entrepreneurial-led families, the focus needs to shift away from the entrepreneur and move toward the family center. The entrepreneur has a limited role and needs to pass the leadership torch to the family team, starting with the family council. The family council will call all the shots, a position that might feel foreign to an entrepreneur. Keep in mind that this transition, this shift in mindset, is difficult for most entrepreneurs to make, but it's not about establishing a new orientation; it's strictly about shifting the leadership for the estate from the entrepreneur to the family.

To change this mindset, bring in professionals skilled in the art and science of conflict resolution, as they can help change behaviors and create a psychologically safe environment. Such a safe environment, first and foremost, requires an outward-looking mindset. The old idiom, "Before you judge a man, walk a mile in his shoes," is about the practice of empathy and understanding at a grassroots level.

Conflict Resolution

Conflict resolution is about preserving the integrity of long-established relationships, which sustains a peaceful and harmonious living environment. To reach this level of harmony and the key to conflict resolution, we must employ active listening. According to the United States Institute of Peace, "Active listening is a way of listening and responding to another person that improves mutual understanding."[4] Engaging in active listening is a learned skill. When we consciously listen, it helps other family members open up about what is important to them. As we ask intentional questions about the other family member's concerns, opportunities, and wants, we can maintain an outward-looking mindset to really "hear" what family members are communicating without judgment or response.

Once you have learned active listening, conflict resolution training helps shift the focus and separate people from the problem. The majority of the time, it is the environment, the processes, and the systems (either formal or informal) that are the root of the problem, not the people involved. By practicing empathy, being open-minded, and maintaining patience, we engender a safe environment

Multigenerational Living

while allowing everyone to express their values, viewpoints, feelings, and frustrations.

Sometimes, however, conflicts can be resolved only with third-party mediation. The story mentioned earlier may have been resolved with this mediation, along with a governance that had been agreed upon by all family members.

Through conflict resolution, family members can develop better communication skills that allow for personal growth through the understanding and appreciation of different perspectives, thereby proactively preventing disagreements that may escalate into more serious issues and allowing your family to live harmoniously on a multigenerational living estate. Aim the process at fostering understanding, respect, and cooperation, with the ultimate goal being the preservation of family bonds and the promotion of a peaceful living environment. Visit MultiGenBook.com for more resources on conflict resolution.

* * *

Once conflict resolution is practiced and understood, your family can now move to the next stage: visioning. The vision process seeks to identify each family member's vision, leading to the establishment of the family's vision statement.

6

Vision

Man plans. God laughs. Recognizing that life's twists and turns come unexpectedly and often at inopportune times reminds us that we have little control over many aspects of our future. Whether you planned, visualized, got the itch, or were inspired to consider multigenerational living is unimportant. What is paramount is how you take action.

Define Your Vision

A vision narrative is the shared purpose and vision of establishing multigenerational living on an estate. Before creating it, though, it's important to complete the critical steps of communication and conflict resolution from Chapters 4 and 5. When your family is ready to communicate effectively within a psychologically safe environment and can listen with empathy and patience, allowing all family members to be heard, only then are you ready to start the vision phase.

In Chapter 1, you read about my journey to living multi-generationally and an example vision narrative.

Multigenerational Living

That narrative we created for our family was the genesis for the first discussions about the possibility of cohabitation, albeit for a few weeks or months at a time. Where we started in our vision of the future and where we ended up turned out to be quite different. We would have saved a tremendous amount of time and effort had we started with trusted communication and conflict resolution. At the time, though, we had no model, no process, and no example to follow. Only through trial and error did we learn much of what you are learning in this book.

The partial vision example in Chapter 1 is repeated here to give you some insight and help to envision why, how, and what your own future might be.

Imagine boarding a helicopter that takes you to the top of the mountain you seek to climb—your multigenerational living facility. You step off the helicopter and look down the mountain to the place you are right now, the present. From your perch on top of the mountain, you can view the easiest, simplest path with the least number of obstacles, switchbacks, and dangerous trail headings to reach the mountain top easily.

Write down in as much detail as possible the vision of living multi-generationally. It may be something like this.

> It's three years from today, _/_/_. My parents, my sister's family, and my family are living multi-generationally. We now live on forty acres with a pond, two streams, and ten acres of tillable fields, along with thirty acres of pristine Colorado mixed evergreen forest. We are five hundred feet in elevation above Denver, a forty-five-minute drive from our new home. There are top-notch hospitals within thirty minutes. The airport is a one-hour drive, providing easy access for periodic business trips along with other travel.

The school district is top-rated, with middle and high schools within a ten-minute drive. My sister's and our children will be attending these schools and are building relationships with other families like ours in the area. All major shopping is within a twenty-minute drive, providing the convenience we desire to keep life as easy and simple as possible. We have eliminated noise and air pollution. It's dark and quiet at night, allowing us to have complete restful sleep, thereby allowing us to start each day off refreshed and eager to meet the day.

We did live in a suburb of Denver to make the short ten-minute daily commute to work. After COVID, we are no longer required to be in the office every day. In fact, my schedule allows me to drive into the office once or twice weekly. My sister and her husband lived in Chicago. They both have jobs that are primarily remote. Once a month, they need to travel to Chicago for business meetings.

The property is awesome! We have three separate homes that are one-minute walking distance apart. There is a fourth building with kitchen facilities that allows us to gather as a family for celebrations, just to break bread or be with each other. One big advantage is we've formed an LLC and Homeowners Association to buy the property and share expenses. Without this arrangement, we would not have been able to purchase and maintain this property.

Early on, we held meetings and went through a formal process of clear communication to establish a stronger, trusted relationship between our families. We discussed and held conflict resolution exercises to get comfortable with uncomfortable situations that will eventually show up in the future.

The original vision statement from above was revised after having each adult family member provide their own vision of their future along with everyone else's. Ultimately, what you see here is an example of what came out of the work we did to come up with a common written vision statement. Unfortunately, this vision narrative is missing what is most important in life for each family member: their purpose, meaning, and vision of their own personal future.

Include Every Person's Vision

To formalize your family's vision of at least one generation into the future (twenty years), you must hear each family member's personal purpose and ensure it becomes part of that shared vision. To gather the necessary information, each family member goes through a process of reflection to answer these questions:

- What is most important in the way you live your life?
- What is really worth doing that you can get behind?
- Deep down, who are you?
- What makes you jump out of bed every morning excited to meet the day head-on?

Once each family member is clear about their vision of the future, you can move forward to formalize a shared family vision statement. The caveat is everyone must feel and be heard. All family members need to be clear about each other's vision statements so that a cohesive and inclusive family vision is formed.

When looking at more established multigenerational estates, this may feel simple. For example, one multigenerational living estate has come a long way from its establishment as a family farm some forty years ago. Initially, it had all the earmarks of a family farm with three generations, along with the typical two to four crops to plant, cultivate, and harvest every year. This entrepreneurial family went much further. They decided to change the way farming is done and became early adopters of regenerative farming. Based on their vision to innovate farming, they have established a farming apprentice program that supports new farming innovations, houses team members, and continually seeks to purchase additional acreage to expand their innovative operations. None of this could have succeeded without multiple generations of family members supporting this shared vision of the future that they are realizing year after year.

As seamless as the process this family did to maintain their vision appears, it's not always easy. Like any new organization, it takes time to get comfortable working and playing together. Our multigenerational family is going through that awkward first phase of realizing our shared family vision. Until recently, we were focused only on sharing vacations and holidays—a much different experience than living the daily grind of life.

Day-to-day living can be difficult, especially when you share it with family members, and you don't know how they operate in different environments, such as when they're under high stress and anxiety. We are a work in progress. We have to remind ourselves to stop and smell the roses—take breaks from each other and from our multigenerational estate.

* * *

Once you've established a shared family vision, almost immediately, the "how to" questions begin. You now have the vision, and you might think the first how-to is about

Multigenerational Living

selecting that "perfect" property, the property with the land, housing, and facilities that support your vision. But not so fast! Before rushing headlong into the emotional rollercoaster of purchasing your estate, you need to set guiding principles, establish boundaries, and organize a family leadership team.

7
Governance

Living in close proximity to another family member can be stressful, frustrating, disconcerting, and even downright awful. The story of the unruly son-in-law is a situation we all want to avoid. By now, you've taken the time to establish and grow trusted relationships with your family members. You now know how to deal with conflicts, hopefully ending with a positive, acceptable result. You've written down your vision, as have each of your family members, and arrived at a shared multigenerational estate vision narrative. Shaping your vision can be a fun, creative time with your family members. But now, we get down to brass tacks.

Governance is a term we usually associate with business entities such as for-profit companies, not-for-profits, or governmental organizations. Realistically, when enough people are involved in operations or attending meetings involving any activity of leisure, hobby, work, or sport, we want to know "the rules." These rules will be the governing documents for your estate.

Organizing Your Governing Documents

The next step is to codify the spirit and underlying values and principles of your family vision into a structure that supports the day-to-day activities, ongoing relationships, and a consensus of what you all believe about multigenerational living on your estate. Guiding family principles will arise almost on a daily basis. That is how important these principles are and why they need to be "etched into stone" and agreed upon by all family members.

This step is not as difficult as it may appear upon first review. You already have all the elements that go into your guiding family principles. Your values and principles have been repeatedly discussed at every step of building the foundation for living multi-generationally. Enlist a professional skilled in this area to help you and your family create and organize your governing documents. This will ensure your structure is thorough and agreeable.

The Seventh Generation Principle

At this point, an important question to answer is how many generations you envision in the future. You may have already answered that question earlier in the process. If not, now is the time.

Consider this the Seventh Generation Principle based on a cultural Iroquois philosophy. It simply states that the decisions you make today should result in a sustainable world seven generations into the future. A baby in an Iroquois community would have to live to see their great-great-grandchild, the seventh generation, to have any connection. Focusing on a future generation that no family member alive will ever meet takes everyone's "agenda" off the table. This ensures the focus is squarely on family values and principles.

On our multigenerational estate, we were faced with a decision to drill a new well because the current well could not meet one of our standard principles of clean, sustainable water. This well would augment the flow and volume of water necessary to comfortably house twenty to twenty-five people, fulfilling all of their water needs. Without this new well, we would violate the seventh generational principle as more families inhabit the property.

We drilled the well.

We had to drill twice as deep as expected to obtain the necessary flow and volume of water. (Next time, we vowed to invest in a water diviner!) The typical well uses a standardized galvanized pipe that eventually leeches lead into the drinking water, which may or may not be removed easily. Stainless steel has no ill effects. We decided to spend an additional $12,000 for a stainless steel pipe to deliver the water from a depth of 758 feet.

The first and second generations will likely not be affected by a newly installed galvanized pipe. However, the third generation could be affected. The decision was made without hesitation. Using the Seventh Generation Principle combined with our guiding principles made this an easy decision. Before living multi-generationally on our estate, we could have easily made the decision to put in the standard galvanized pipe with the understanding the next owners or the ones after them would deal with any possible leaching issues.

Values matter. Principles matter. Vision matters.

Answer this question: What must be true for your beliefs, values, and principles to be adhered to and acted upon on a daily basis?

The answer to this question will go a long way in putting together your governance for multigenerational living on your estate.

Choose Your Governing Leadership

What makes up the governance of your estate? Formally, it's establishing the bylaws and the operating charter. An operating charter is a formal written agreement defining the roles, responsibilities, and expectations of each family member. As part of establishing the bylaws and operating charter, you must select a multigenerational council typically composed of the family members who make up the current leadership of the multigenerational estate. Typically, one generation is "in charge" but not "in control." They have accepted and taken on the responsibility for all decision-making for the multigenerational living estate.

Let's be clear about what the terms *in charge and in control* mean. One of the first lessons in leadership I learned as a brand-new Infantry Second Lieutenant at West Point was that my Platoon Sergeant was *in control* at all times in the Garrison and in the field. As officers, we were *in charge* in Garrison and in the field. These roles had clear and distinct duties and responsibilities. In Garrison, we had little to do, mostly attending lots of meetings and planning. The sergeants and enlisted soldiers executed the plans. Corporate America operates similarly as the leaders or executives do little legwork.

We see the same in a multigenerational estate. The majority of the work is accomplished by those *not* on the multigenerational council. The multigenerational living council is the decision-making authority, not the micromanager. They're not the ones holding everything up while everyone waits for their decision. If the council tries to be in charge and in control, it places those doing the work in an order-taker role. Generally, it is difficult to work in an environment where someone with less knowledge is dictating how to do a job. Instead, those doing the work—family members, vendors, and hired help—will be more successful if they have control over their work and working environment and take the lead on the task or project. As a good friend of mine reminds me, you can't be in "ConCharge," that is, in control and in charge.

Personal vs. Multigenerational Ownership on an Estate

Another key differentiator is the rule of law regarding asset ownership. Each family member will have assets owned individually, jointly, in trust, in retirement accounts, and so on. Family members will have personal property and vehicles. Multigenerational living governance may address how motorized or non-motorized vehicles or equipment may be utilized on the property. Are there specific areas for parking? Will you have rules on traversing the estate or where activities take place? Multigenerational living governance does not address the actual ownership of the facility itself. Nor will it address how the deeds are titled and how those titles change ownership based on disability, death, or incompetence. Those issues are controlled by appropriately structured estate planning documents.

Limited Liability Companies (LLCs), corporations, trusts, or other entities may own the property based on how the family decides to fund and operate the multigenerational living estate. We will cover this in later chapters. Governance will address education, training, and mentoring the upcoming generations. Remember, studies have shown that 24 percent of families do not survive three generations due to their failure to prepare future generations. They were not provided the "tools" necessary to operate the multigenerational estate and to successfully accept, operate, and grow the assets passed on to them from the older generations.

Multigenerational Living

You may wonder who will draft these documents. If your family is not willing to put the governance documents together due to lack of time, expertise, or experience, then hire a professional—an attorney, consultant, or other advisor who specializes in these types of documents—to do so. Regardless of who crafts the documents, all family members will need to review and accept them. All adult family members will sign off on these documents, indicating their commitment to the organizing principle guidelines, rules, and boundaries set forth under the operation of the multigenerational living estate.

Many families have different definitions of an adult. Some families have gone so far as to not release their estate assets until their children are of retirement age for fear of them losing the will and purpose to work for a living. Generally, age 21 is the legal age for an adult. This is one of those areas where families have to decide when a member living on the estate signs their intention to abide by the governance of the estate. Some families may have junior estate members who begin to take on responsibilities at the age of 12 or younger. Think of this like chores being assigned to children.

Once you and your family are committed to living multi-generationally and have completed this critical foundational setup, you're now ready for the next stage, where you'll select and purchase your property.

STAGE TWO
Structure

8

Structure

Many years ago when I was starting my business, I would make a weekly trip to Downtown Chicago to meet with prospective clients. I would park in the outer "loop" parking lots to save money and walk into the city.

Invariably, there were new building projects under various stages of construction along my way. Construction noise boomed from a few stories below ground where crews were pile-driving pylons and doing other foundational work. This would continue on any given property for what seemed like an inordinately long time, usually about six months, until one day, two or three floors of steel girders would magically appear from behind the fence. Within weeks, the building jumped skyward as if the project finally appeared to be taking off.

During the first stage of setting up multigenerational living on your estate, your family put in the quality time and effort to establish a foundation to last seven generations or more. On the surface, it appears that little was accomplished toward establishing your estate. However, as we see in the construction of a multistory building, living multi-generationally requires principle pylons with deep roots, your agreed-upon family purpose, and a vision of the future.

There are critical questions to consider in this stage:

- Who will be living on the property?
- What are the non-negotiables and negotiables utilized in selecting the property?
- How will the ownership and finances operate?
- What is the timeline?
- Will the property be existing or built after purchasing raw land?
- What historical, charitable, conservation, municipal, and governmental easements, along with HOA restrictions or other limiting legal arrangements, are acceptable to your family?
- Will there be single or multiple business(es) or charitable operations and their form of ownership?
- Does the property have acceptable water/well, sewer/septic, internet, and other necessary utilities?

These and many other questions you may have about property selection—or eliminating unacceptable properties—will come up in this stage. Be prepared to think through the variety of ways to go through that selection or elimination process.

The following stage of the estate transformation will add all the features and the "beauty" of your facility, much like adding the walls, windows, floors, ceilings, and other beautiful finished work.

Strengthen Family Bonds

Structure matters, and what provides a strong structure is strong familial bonds. It is the most important element in forming your multigenerational living situation. When the family is hunkered down and weathering bad times, such as the death of a loved one, financial woes, or other difficult transitions, the family structure holds everything together.

Our family has long believed that clean water, clean air, wholesome nutrition, sun, adequate sleep, and exercise are the core basics for living a healthy life, so having a core principle of supplying clean water at all times seems like a given. Drilling a new, much deeper well with safer construction materials drives home the application of that principle in practice. That decision was not a given.

One of the families we interviewed has a family principle to invite people into their home on a weekly basis to create a connection and share their life with them. They extended this core family principle when viewing how and what to do on their multigenerational living property. One of the ways they have permanently applied this family principle is to have an event site on their property hosting local bands for weekend concerts everyone can enjoy.

What can your family do to strengthen bonds? Take time to write down some ideas and share those with the other family members.

Define Your Principles

Family principles are non-negotiable. They are your family's right reason and right purpose. They will not be violated under any circumstance. Family principles will define the form of structure for your family. They will drive the discussion and selection of the physical property you will consider to support those principles. A music venue requires a more rural location with enough land to comfortably house the family, the venue, and the supporting infrastructure and team to successfully operate the venue.

In this stage, much like you had discussions about your family's values, you'll define your non-negotiables and negotiables about your future property. You will be introduced to a decision-making process that doesn't conform to mainstream ideas—Corporate America's boardrooms and standards don't adhere to the discernment or consensus approach. First, you will establish a short-term ideal to capture the opportunity to find the right property. Before making the purchase, you will conduct a financial stress test to ensure the successful purchase and operation of your multigenerational living estate. This will naturally lead to the proper ownership and structure of your estate to support your family's vision of the future.

* * *

The next chapter will start off with an approach you may have experienced in the first stage: discerning each family member's roles, duties, and responsibilities, along with reaching a consensus when making important multigenerational decisions.

9

From Discernment to Consensus

Corporate America has adopted a common approach to assessing what a company does best now and in the future. This approach is a SWOT analysis, which stands for Strengths, Weaknesses, Opportunities, and Threats. A SWOT analysis helps break down and analyze a company's current state to determine what leadership should immediately focus on to continue the growth of the company.

However, your family is not a company boardroom whose role is to grow a company without regard to the principles and purpose of its leaders and employees. The saying, "It's just business," doesn't apply here. That approach permanently burns bridges and destroys the trust developed diligently over time between and among family members.

Discernment and Unique Ability®

Discernment is a process for making decisions that takes in the wisdom of outside sources to open yourself to forming decisions that are in the best interest of you and your family. In the past, you may have used this process. Some will use this approach to gain spiritual enlightenment through meditation or spiritual practices to determine what they believe they are called to do.

Bringing this process to the ground level, we use the term Unique Ability, a tool devised by Strategic Coach®, to help entrepreneurs and their teams determine the best use of each individual's unique talent, wisdom, and skills. You may think that Unique Ability can be difficult to identify, but usually, you use it so effortlessly that you don't see it. Others do. The process of discernment helps bring each family member's Unique Ability to the surface when others recognize and communicate the importance of each family member doing what they do uniquely well. We generally love operating in our Unique Ability even though we may not be aware of exactly what our Unique Ability is.

The discernment process allows everyone to have a voice based on their view of family principles and how they apply them on a daily basis. This subtle approach ferrets out the true essence of what makes each of us want to pursue our purpose for our own personal "right reason." This is the time when you will select (discern), assign, and accept duties, roles, and responsibilities. That leads us to the second half of the discernment process—where the group reaches a consensus about these roles, duties, and responsibilities.

Consensus and Discernment

Consensus means coming to an agreement. Creating consensus in a multigenerational situation means finding common ground that everyone can support with no opposition. The first time going through consensus can be difficult, especially for the entrepreneur who is used to having the final say, because this approach moves the decision-making from one or more people to the entire family. This is not a democratic approach where a majority vote-getter wins. And this is not about the meeting after the meeting, you know, that invisible meeting where a personal agenda-driven approach makes the "real" decision outside of the meeting. In this process, much like nine members of a jury, everyone must agree on the decision. It's important to note that it's not necessary for all family members to entirely agree with the decision as long as they support the decision that allows the family to move forward. This is consensus.

A natural outcome of discernment, when we apply it to the real-world issue of selecting a multigenerational living situation, is that one or more of the family principles may come into question. There may need to be a deeper understanding and application of one or more of your family principles. Discernment creates a different lens of discovery that you may not have seen when going through the trusted communication, conflict resolution, and visioning stages. We don't want to hold the family's feet to the fire concerning the selected principles; rather, we work with family members as they learn to understand the application of a family principle.

The entrepreneur may find the discernment process difficult and disconcerting. The rhythm and flow of the process are different than what they're accustomed to, and they no longer have the ability to alter a decision. The whole process seems foreign after spending the majority of their working years yielding the authority to change on the dime, reverse decisions, and even abandon years of work. If you find this process too difficult to navigate on your own, consider hiring a facilitator to smooth out the rough edges of change.

The facilitator is the go-between. When we were starting our process, I'd seen enough entrepreneurs permanently damage relationships through their bull-in-a-china shop approach to family members who are uncomfortable with risk-taking, change, and uncertainty. To not injure our family relationships, I had to get out of my own way. We needed a facilitator because my strength as an entrepreneur was a weakness from a family perspective. I tended to be so forceful and blunt that family members remained quiet, not participating in the discussions, when I was "on." Fortunately my wife and I recognized I needed someone impartial and experienced to facilitate my involvement in our family meetings. We agreed that whatever the facilitator said to do, we would, regardless of my initial thoughts.

You may think this discernment process comes across as more socialistic than democratic. Our democracy is based on our country's strong rule of law with clearly defined human freedoms. Discernment and consensus work as a subset of our democratic society when we address the human wants and needs of a family unit. This works for families, family groups, and community groups.

This is important because an up or down vote, especially on a contentious issue, is certain to alienate some family members. The governance provides the boundaries, the bumper guards, to allow every family member to play anywhere between the lines. This seems as if we are restricting the freedoms of family members, but it is just the opposite. Reaching consensus preserves family relationships, which is integral to living multi-generationally.

A Caveat for Entrepreneurs

The majority of entrepreneurs are attracted to the entrepreneurial lifestyle because they believe it will afford them more freedom. That is true only if they exercise their authority to enjoy those freedoms. Many entrepreneurs are boundaryless. They have not established appropriate boundaries between work and home, thereby making their life chaotic and leaving those around them feeling frustrated. As a result, everyone feels powerless.

Imagine for a moment there is a square shaped playground with four roads on each side with no stop signs or traffic lights. There is no fence around the playground separating it from the dangerous flow of non-stop traffic. The playground has play equipment in the center and also in various locations around the outside of the playground. The children on the playground are only utilizing the play equipment in the center of the playground to not wander to close to the busy roads for fear of injury or loss of life. Such is the life of many entrepreneurs. A misunderstanding of how to utilize their newfound freedom.

Now imagine a tall, impenetrable fence is constructed on all four sides of the playground to ensure that no child can wander into the busy thoroughfares. All of a sudden, the children are spreading out throughout the playground, interacting with new playground equipment and forming new experiences.

This is the freedom afforded when setting appropriate boundaries. Entrepreneurs must set up new boundaries on their multigenerational living estates to experience and allow family members to experience their newly established multigenerational lives fully. They may still run their business with their respective boundaries, but their new boundaries will prohibit them from wreaking havoc on their families.

The formation of your multigenerational living estate may be set up so that everyone agrees up front that the discernment and consensus decision-making model is the necessary approach to successfully growing your estate. You certainly don't have to use discernment and consensus. However, after working with many families over thirty-plus years, we find it is a viable alternative to the typical majority-wins decision-making model.

* * *

Chapter 10 jumps right into how to determine your family's negotiables and non-negotiables as the guidelines and boundaries to clarify these important elements that make up the basis for your property selection.

10

Process of Elimination

At the elemental level, the process of elimination is what we were taught in algebra class. We determined which variable was to be eliminated, then proceeded to either add or subtract to simplify the equation and solve for x. Yes, this is a shortened version; however, I'll bore you with no more painful math references for now.

Emotional Impact

You may recall the story of the Sirens as relayed in Homer's Odyssey. Odysseus, a great warrior, was returning home after the Trojan War. He spent ten years wandering with his ship and crew before he made it home. At one point, he realized they were approaching the island that was home to the Sirens. Supposedly, they sang so beautifully that their songs would lure sailors to their shore, where they would kill them.

Odysseus wanted to hear the Sirens' song but not be lured into the island. He instructed his crew to place beeswax in their ears and lash him to the mast of the ship so he could not get loose. He also instructed them that no matter how much he begged to be released, they were to ignore him and sail safely past the island. As the ship passed the Sirens, Odysseus was beside himself and begged and begged for his men to release him. They did not, and once they safely passed the island, Odysseus was released unharmed.

You probably don't have to go to such an extreme as Odysseus when selecting a property. However, there will come a time when a family member becomes so infatuated by an inappropriate property that you will have to help them through the decision not to select that particular property. The emotion of the moment is instinctive. However, we are not defined by our initial reaction to any emotion. It is in our nature to be moved emotionally. Otherwise, we would just be machines, or like Spock on Star Trek—not emotional, only logical.

We can all agree that buying a property for a nuclear family is an emotional event. But buying a property with multiple families for multigenerational living is *very* emotional. We want everything to be perfect with your "forever home." This a term many use to mean that place you will inhabit until you are removed in a pine box. For your multigenerational living estate, this "forever home" is for the next seven generations, not just for you. We dream of being swept across the threshold into the welcoming arms of our mystical, fantastic property.

Hold on a second. We know it doesn't work this way. There's a good chance we'll make a poor choice in selecting a property and may be eagerly awaiting the day they can sell the property to search for the right-fit property again. Research has shown that the majority of the decisions we make (70 to 90 percent, depending on the study) we make using emotion. We are persuaded by reason, but

Multigenerational Living

we are moved by emotion. Afterward, when asked why we purchased the property, we rationalize our actions to ourselves and to others.

When I was much younger and not very well-formed about money, I got carried away buying a car. At that time, I was jealous of what I perceived as everyone around me driving nice high-end BMW, Mercedes, Lexus, and other luxury vehicles. We were barely meeting our expenses as we were building our business from the ground up. I needed a car, a "new" car.

I walked into a car dealership and was immediately attracted to a very nice sports car. *I've got to have it. I can't afford it. I've got to have it. I can't afford it.* My emotions got the best of me, resulting in driving out of that dealership with a brand new, very expensive sports car. I immediately dreaded owning that vehicle. My happiest times owning that vehicle occurred twice: the five minutes immediately after purchasing the sports car and the day I sold it two years later and bought a very affordable used vehicle. This is a classic story about emotional decision-making. Thankfully, lesson learned, and hopefully not ever to be repeated.

When you completed your vision narrative, your family selected the principles and values that represented who you are as a family. Your principles have become your right reason and your right purpose. When you keep those in mind when you start your process of elimination on potential properties, you have a better chance of making a wise decision that is not based on emotions.

Negotiables vs. Non-Negotiables

Before ever looking at a property, your family must determine your *needs* (non-negotiables) and your *wants* (negotiables). On Maslow's hierarchy of needs, we must fulfill our physiological and security needs before we can move up the ladder to the higher-level needs of belonging, self-esteem, and self-actualization.

Your base pyramid of needs for your property, derived primarily from the principles and values of your vision narrative, may not be violated. All must be present on the property. These needs make up your non-negotiable list.

During our family discussions, we kindly reminded one another of our non-negotiable list that we would not violate. The property must have these attributes/features, or else the family can't move forward to our extended family's pyramid of hierarchy. The list needn't be long. We had a list of six items. Several properties missed just one of these features. We wished the property had the one missing feature, but there was no way to include it, no matter how much money or other efforts we made on our part. The must-haves list is inviolable.

On the other hand, your wants list can be as long as you wish. These wants are your negotiables. This is the point at which you'll want to apply the 80/20 rule. This 80/20 rule is not Pareto's principle; Strategic Coach introduced this altered version to me. Basically, no matter when you begin anything new, you will only get 80 percent of it right the first time. No matter how much preparation, research, discovery, or any other preparatory part, the result will be the same. You will achieve the first 80 percent.

For example, if you have a list of fifteen negotiable features for your property, only 80 percent of them need to be present or may be required upon purchasing the property. With fifteen items, twelve have to be there. We can accept missing a few negotiables because the perfect property doesn't exist. To begin this process, meet with all your family members and develop your master list. Use some of the techniques you learned in Chapters 4 and 5 on communication and conflict resolution.

By combining everyone's needs and wants, you will have a master list. Use consensus to finalize this list and get buy-in from all appropriate family members. Break down the overall list into non-negotiables and negotiables. Anytime one of your family members is having an Odysseus moment, to quiet the Siren song playing in their head, you may quietly remind them of how everyone agreed on the specific non-negotiables.

Now that you have finalized the master list, you have one of the key elements necessary to begin your search.

Selection Criteria

Before getting to the selection criteria, let's talk about the process of selection. Consider a large human resources department searching for a new executive to hire. They will go through a seven- or eight-step selection process. They look at the candidates' formal education and job experience after carefully analyzing the required skills and job description. Then, they select and interview suitable candidates. Finally, an appropriate candidate is selected, accepted, and onboarded into the new job.

Alternatively, interviewing for a spouse from a number of candidates who meet your "job" description is hardly feasible. Instead, most of our potential spousal candidates are eliminated because they have attributes we can't live with. When the "right one" comes along we accept them and begin a life together. We don't let "perfect" be the enemy of good. Just like there is no perfect spouse, there is no perfect property.

During the process of finding properties, you will eliminate the majority because they don't meet certain non-negotiable criteria. This can help you eliminate many properties before even selecting one to visit. Keep in mind that larger multigenerational properties can be like little towns with all the infrastructure, good and bad, that comes with the property and can take a full day to visit and vet. The property itself may be problematic with non-desirable easements, faulty design, irreparable features, or other faults based on your criteria. It is much easier to walk away from a phenomenal, beautiful property if you know in advance what your multifamily priorities are and that one does not meet one of your non-negotiable attributes.

Time and Emotion Will Affect Everyone

You may wonder, after weeks or months of searching, whether you will ever find your right-fit property. Not to worry. As my grandmother, who never drove a car, used to say, "There is always another street car." Over time, I found this to be true. We have had that experience in the many properties we've owned over the years. When one property was out of reach monetarily or otherwise, sure enough, a better property would surface.

Another important aspect is that when using the family principles to look for properties, the process of elimination negates the emotional highs and lows. When one family is gaga about a property, the others help to ease them through their disappointment by reiterating the reasons it does not meet your selected criteria. Searches can be for land with appropriate natural features or with all or most of the required infrastructure already in place, but it can take a long time, especially if the criteria are specific. Even though our area of concentration was 2,100 square miles across three states, it still took a lot of patience and time as we combed through hundreds of properties in search of our right-fit property.

Multigenerational Living

* * *

The following chapter reviews how to conduct a financial stress test for your multigenerational family, another potentially emotionally driven element that can financially turn your multigenerational estate upside down.

11

Financial Stress Test

Your family has bought into the idea of multigenerational living, you've created a vision, and now you're eager to find that special property. Knowing how much you have in savings and cash, as well as in future income, is imperative before you make that purchase. A financial stress test helps you determine the maximum purchase price and ongoing operational expenses of your multigenerational living estate. Many properties struggle, are sold, or are simply abandoned for lack of long-term cash flow stability.

The mortgage part of the purchase is actually the most straightforward part of the transaction. The PITI (principal, interest, taxes, and insurance) covers the overall capital expenditure and the annual real estate and insurance expenses. Real estate taxes and insurance expenses generally go up due to inflation over time. They are easier to plan going forward.

For example, a $2 million property with 20 percent down yields a $1.6 million mortgage; at 5 percent for thirty years, it costs $8,589 monthly. Assuming $24,000

Multigenerational Living

of real estate taxes and $6,000 of homeowner's coverage, the monthly total is $11,089 monthly or $133,068 on an annual basis. In this example, contributing individuals will cover these expenses from their incomes after taxes.

One note about real estate taxes. When families decide to farm or conduct other agricultural activities, they may file for an agricultural exemption with the local municipality. There are strict requirements to maintain the agricultural exemption on that portion of the estate used for this purpose. Generally, real estate is valued in two parts. The livable portion of the entire property is valued as normal, with one acre or so of land associated with that space. The remaining acreage is valued as farmland at a much lower rate.

Non-Traditional Funding

Buying a multigenerational estate is a much more complex transaction than that of a single-family residence. There is a very good possibility that the traditional mortgage for single-family homes will not be available for such a property transaction. You will most likely need to seek funding from non-traditional financing resources. These non-traditional funding companies may require an interest rate premium and a more commercial-line approach to financing, something like a twenty-year amortized note that adjusts after five years and has a 1 to 2 percent interest rate premium. In the above example, the prevailing rate of 5 percent may have a 2 percent additional premium added to this "non-conventional" loan. The monthly payment for a $1.6 million, 7 percent, twenty-year amortized note is $12,405.

The income required to service the PITI In this example is an earned income of around $270,000. The underwriting for this mortgage may require 30 percent down and at least two years of $600,000 plus annual income. The underwriting financial lender may require additional proof of other investable assets, which may be satisfied by investment real estate, 401(k)s, IRAs, or other liquid non-retirement accounts.

Let's assume you, the entrepreneur, won't be solely responsible for funding and operating your property. As we saw above, it is more complicated when pooling resources to purchase and operate a multigenerational living property. Having multiple buyers will require some creativity in the purchase. Most likely, the underwriter will require cross-collateralization (all owners have their assets collateralized in the transaction) to accept the risk of underwriting the note (mortgage).

Legal Entities and Funding

You may form a homeowner's association (HOA) or other legal entity to pay all the costs for the estate. Each family occupying the property must determine their monthly/annual contribution toward this HOA. Every family involved must go through the painful process of budgeting. Don't let that discourage you—it is not as hard as it first appears. Let's break down the costs.

To start, the current operating costs to run each family's current living arrangement may be assumed when coming up with the property's maximum purchase price and the property's monthly operating expenses. The operating costs to calculate include but are not limited to:

- real estate loan/taxes/insurance
- utilities
- exterior and interior maintenance
- repairs

- well
- septic
- propane/gas

These are the major joint expenses that each family will pay as part of the overall expenses.

You may not have experienced servicing a well for drinking water, a septic field, or refilled propane tanks if you've only lived in an urban/suburban environment. These self-maintained utilities have their own set of monthly expenses, repair, and capital expenditures. In most places, well water needs to be analyzed for lead, sulfates, and harmful bacteria and minerals. Treatment systems are generally installed that may put your water through two to five phases of filtering, cleaning, and other requirements based on the quality of the water. Like us, you may need to drill a new well when adding more people to a property that earlier serviced fewer families.

The same is true for additional septic fields. Generally, septic fields are sized by the number of bedrooms per household property. Any changes/additional bedrooms may require new septic fields or replacements. Recent regulations may require more expensive setups (for example, mound systems in low-percolation environments).

In northern climates, larger properties will require snow removal and ice treatment on roadways that may reach a mile in total length. This can be quite expensive, depending on the frequency and amount of snowfall. Many properties require days, not hours, to cut grass or maintain landscaping. You may need one or more full-time staff to handle all the seasonal maintenance and repair. It is not unusual to have annual expenses of $50,000 to $150,000 for staff, depending on the size and complexity of the property.

In an earlier chapter, we reviewed the Unique Ability of family members occupying the estate. As an example, you may decide to purchase snow removal equipment that attaches to a truck or farm tractor to remove snow and treat ice using a family member's time and effort. Consider what "chores" family members may perform and those that will be hired out. In addition, each individual family must divide their monthly expenses between estate and personal expenses to arrive at their total outlay.

One caveat: One of the biggest and most variable monthly expenses can be maintenance and repair, especially for older properties. The older the property, the greater the expenses.

Three Factors to a Healthy Financial Estate

The financial stress test is a review of your estate and each family's cash flow, taxes, and balance sheet. These are the three key financial indicators of an overall financially healthy multigenerational living estate. Consider hiring a financial adviser who specializes in analyzing and advising on how to perform a financial stress test.

Cash Flow

Cash flow is the main driver in operating your multigenerational living property. If, after performing the financial stress test, the family members determine they may collectively contribute $20,000 monthly, then a mock-up property value along with operating costs may be determined before going out and finding a property. (The $20,000 is a net income number. It's derived after the government withholds all taxes and other employment benefits.) If family members are actively working, they may be contributing to a 401k (balance sheet growth) along with Social Security, Medicare, state taxes, federal taxes, healthcare, and other miscellaneous expenses. It is not unusual to be grossing

Multigenerational Living

$200,000 of active employment income with a take-home net of $120,000 annually. This $120,000 must cover estate operating expenses along with personal expenses. Using this example, you have only $48,000 annually, or $4,000 monthly, available for the estate's operating expenses.

Eventually, family members retire. They will then live off pensions, Social Security, and income from their balance sheet assets. As an example, the balance sheet to support a $2-million multigenerational living estate when everyone contributing to property expenses is retired may call for a collective $10 million of investable assets to generate the necessary income to operate the property.

Taxes

Each individual family member will have their own tax picture. During active employment, taxes are higher due to the current 7.65 percent Social Security withholding that goes away at retirement. State, local, and federal taxes will most likely be reduced in retirement. To make certain your family estate will operate successfully, each family must calculate their personal and estate budget along with projecting when they may retire to continue to support those necessary expenses.

Balance Sheet

The overall multigenerational living projection is a combination of all the collective income and overall property expenses. A mock multigenerational living projection may be illustrated to then back into the purchase price and operating expenses for your future multigenerational facility.

Yes, you'll need professional assistance at this point unless you have a family member who has the appropriate software to determine taxes and cash flow accurately now and throughout a projection. Coaching each family member through the various aspects of pre- and post-retirement cash flow, balance sheet, and tax planning is necessary to complete the financial stress test.

* * *

Good news! You've passed the financial stress test. In Chapter 12, we'll delve into how to own your multigenerational living estate. The traditional forms of ownership, joint tenancy or tenancy by the entirety, don't work well when considering multiple owners of an estate property.

12

The Estate Structure

A famous American philosopher and jurist, the Honorable Learned Hand, sat on the First Circuit Court of New York in the 1930s and 1940s. One of his many words of wisdom as a judge was, "In America, there are two tax systems, one for the informed and one for the uninformed."[5] We want to be in the informed camp. As mentioned earlier, the structure selected to own your multigenerational living estate will stand or not stand based on the estate's structure—how well you devise, develop, and form it and how well succeeding generations prudently manage it.

The Importance of Estate Structure

You must be clear and certain about the structure's form, who the parties are, and who is responsible for the estate's successful function and operation. Those individuals need to adequately address and comply with the cash flow, balance sheet, and taxes for your multigenerational estate.

Your estate structure, the form of ownership chosen, drives the flow of money in and through your estate. When your estate is small, let's say less than $5 million, then the long-term structure is not as critical as it is for larger estates.

Generally, a multigenerational living estate will not be formed by most middle-American families; there is not enough wealth or annual cash flow to successfully operate one. However, we do see it being accomplished on the traditional family farms that survived the Industrial Revolution. These are DIY family farms with three or four generations who spend the majority of their time in cash crops, dairy, or other farming activities. They are all-in and have many generations of institutional family knowledge and experience living on their family farm.

For those not on a multigenerational family farm, the mid-level estate will be supported by a net worth of generally $5 to $20 million, with over $500,000 of annual income to support its annual operations. It's also important to set aside an emergency fund to support one full year of operations. In the earlier example, that is about $200,000. You should have another 3–5 years ($600,000–$1 million) available beyond that amount to financially weather a five-year rough patch.

It is ill-advised for an entrepreneur to be the financial backer of the estate and run this operation because entrepreneurs are notorious for throwing all their chips in to capture various new opportunities. This doesn't provide stability for your estate. Instead, at least a minimum amount of assets must be set aside to allow for the survival of the property in the event of a total financial collapse of other entrepreneurial opportunities.

One early lesson in my wealth management career was learning where to place the primary emphasis when working with clients—current living or death planning? In your planning, should the emphasis be on current cash flow, balance sheet, and taxes or placed on the formation of the estate upon the death of the patriarch or matriarch? The current living planning takes the first position. Without the appropriate structure for current operations, you'll have no need to address the passing of assets at death.

Ownership and Control

Ultimately, the estate structure primarily focuses on passing assets to the next generation. Typically, the wills/trusts/entities you create will be etched into stone once one of the initial wealth builders dies. Therefore, the overall structure, legal language, tax structure(s), and rights and powers of the beneficiaries need to be carefully discerned through seventh-generation philosophical thinking.

Most estates use some sort of revocable trust instrument to take ownership of the estate. In the case of multiple families owning a property, that structure may entail other legal entities (LLCs, corporations, partnerships). Whatever form you select, you must tailor it to fit the family's operations, the families' individual estate structure, and ownership of the multigenerational living estate.

In some situations involving larger estates, this is the time to consider how to transfer ownership and control to future generations. Some of the ownership may be transferred upfront while maintaining control of most of the decision-making. The goal is to move growth-type assets—the multigenerational living property—to the next generation now by transferring only the ownership. Meanwhile, the first generation maintains control over most of the decision-making. You may transfer the decision-making control at some future point before death or at the death of the patriarch or matriarch to allow the younger generations to take over the reins of ownership.

By transferring the wealth part now, it allows that part of the estate to grow tax-free, no matter its growth rate or future value. Doing so allows the estate to remain intact and not subject to transfer taxes (taxes upon the death when passing assets to non-spouses), such as federal estate tax, state estate tax, or state inheritance tax. I know, those are lots of taxes.

Currently, there is a lifetime tax exemption available to couples that exceed $20 million. This exemption may be used during life by filing a gift tax return (no tax due), thereby giving notice to the IRS of the transfer. This is the sort of action that may be taken to remove assets from your estate to avoid the estate taxes of a much larger estate in the future. (The tax code is an ever-changing creature that may be beneficial in one generation but disastrous in another as it is controlled by the whims, winds, and illogical nature of Congress from administration to administration.) Once assets are removed, they stay removed and are not subject to these onerous taxes in the future.

Estate taxes destroy estates. One of the most famous stories is that of the Joe Robbie family, owners of the Miami Dolphins up through the early 90s. The family was reported to have paid $47 million in estate taxes after Joe Robbie's death. This was because he owned all the assets in his estate, including the Miami Dolphins football franchise. The family was forced to sell the Miami Dolphins, thereby losing the jewel of their family to raise the necessary cash to pay the estate taxes. A sad story that could have ended differently had the family addressed the tax issue well before Joe Robbie's death.

Another example is the fortuitous death of George Steinbrenner (at least from a tax perspective), the owner of the New York Yankees baseball franchise. He died in 2010, the only year in recent history with no estate tax, due to a wrinkle in the estate tax laws at the time. His estate supposedly saved $600 million in estate taxes. Unbelievable!

Asset Removal

You may be growing your business rapidly and thereby growing your estate. At some point, removing assets from your estate may also be fortuitous. Legal and accounting counsel may be necessary to look at the appropriate options available for estate planning. Whether your estate structure is single-family or multifamily, all families will want to have wills/trusts in place to properly transfer their assets to the next generation(s). Multi-family ownership is a little more involved in how ownership and control pass, especially if one family wants to leave the multigenerational living situation or another family wants to join.

Several clauses in the governing documents may allow for some kind of a buy-and-sell arrangement and the right of first refusal. In plain English, if and when a family wants to sell their ownership stake in the property, the other families are allowed to buy it, or if another family wants to come onto the estate, they could buy the interest from the departing family.

No matter the process you select to easily transfer ownership, you include it in a manner that's acceptable to the principles and values of the family and meets the non-negotiables of the families as well.

Like many of the stages in the process of living multi-generationally on your estate, there is much more to the estate and financial structure of such a property than is covered here. Keep the lines of communication open with all family members as you develop your estate's structure and use professional assistance when needed.

*　*　*

The last chapter in this stage is to review the timeline as part of the overall selection and purchase of the multi-generational estate. Now, we'll refine your vision of living multi-generationally on your estate with this newfound information.

13

Timeline and Selection Criteria

The Chinese philosopher Lao Tzu once said, "The journey of a thousand miles begins with a single step." By this point in your journey to living on a multi-family estate, it probably already feels like you're well on your way to covering that thousand miles. We've reached the really exciting and fun leg of the journey. It is also the most emotionally frustrating and anxious part. However, you and your family are well-prepared if you have gone through and addressed each part of these two stages.

You've already accomplished all the foundational work that forms the basis of all future decision-making. Your family has built trusted communication and knows how to resolve the inevitable conflicts. Your family has determined the form of ownership and the leadership team who will head up the search for your multigenerational living estate. You have already determined price points and annual cash flow requirements to successfully operate the estate over the long term. Most importantly, you have a clear, crisp vision of the future backed by family values and principles that determine the non-negotiable and negotiable elements to successfully guide your search to find your right-fit multigenerational living estate. Before finding and completing the purchase of the property, it is now appropriate to determine your search parameters and a timeline.

Setting the Closing Date

One key action to take before you start searching for the property is to determine the actual date when you will close on your multigenerational living estate. No matter the difficulty in selecting that date, it must be decided upon and placed on your calendar, to-do list, or other organizational tool you use. Without an end date, your search can easily lose energy and momentum. Earl Monroe, a former professional NBA player, said, "Be quick, but don't hurry." Make this your call to action. The date may be determined by other factors, such as selling other family properties to have the money for a down payment and being right side up on your expenses.

You may not agree with my next piece of advice; however, it will hasten your search and make it much less stressful. Sell the property any family member lives on before buying your multigenerational living estate. There are two reasons for this methodology. First and most important, you'll have cash on hand to immediately structure the best transaction possible. Remember, you are purchasing your forever home. The sooner each family member jettisons their old home, the more relaxed and focused you will be on finding your right fit.

The second reason is stark and effective. It plays on the same reasoning Hernán Cortés used in 1519 when he instructed his 60-man crew to burn all their boats upon landing in the New World. By selling those houses, you will have their complete commitment to finding and purchasing your multigenerational living estate. Compare this to the relationship of the pig and the chicken to the bacon-and-eggs breakfast. The pig is committed, but the chicken merely participates. No chickens are allowed on this transformational family journey.

Define Your Search Parameters

Once you've selected a date and locked it in, you may start the search parameters. Our search started very broadly with a very "soft" acquisition date—we thought it could be a decade before we purchased a property. We looked at properties from southern Maine to northern North Carolina, along and near the Appalachian range. We had no budget, but we had a vague notion as to our price point—it was an ineffectual approach. It took four years! We knew better, but we had little guidance on this massive project. Eventually, we narrowed our search to a 2,100-square-mile area across three states with a goal of not being further than an hour's drive from the northern Washington, DC, area.

We were open to building on raw land or buying an existing property, and we had selected a price point range. We did have our non-negotiables and negotiables. We had a core leadership team of two families that met frequently once the process sped up during the beginning of COVID-19. The timeline and existing property sales lined up well. Luckily, our first two contracts fell through because our third contract was on our current property, which met all our non-negotiables and the majority of our negotiables. It fulfilled and continues to fulfill all our family principles, values, and purpose. We were fortunate to get this one right with little guidance other than my experience helping families establish their multigenerational financial and estate structures.

You'll need a few specialists to help in your search. Look for real estate professionals who specialize in larger multigenerational properties. They are few and far between. They need to be local experts on land, community, infrastructure, and municipal issues particular to your search area. There are real estate professionals who specialize in land purchases. Again, they are few in number but worth their weight in gold.

Depending on where you are in your search priorities, you may have to set two dates. One date to finalize your search area and one to complete the transaction. During the first two years, we ruled out everything north of Maryland and south of Northern Virginia. We narrowed our search area by visiting properties and raw land possibilities. Many of your search parameters will arise from your non-negotiables and negotiables along with meeting your values, principles, and purpose/vision. You may have strict guidelines for the size of acreage, minimum livable home space, number of residences, type and mixture of land with particular features, and a host of other requirements related to your established criteria.

We hired several real estate agents to work across our search area, one being much more proactive than the others, while we conducted our own separate searches on the internet. One very important caveat: on the East Coast, many larger properties have established easements. These may be historical (many Civil War battlefields in our area), conservation, municipal, state, or federal, along with utility and more. The majority of properties we found to be suitable failed due to restrictions in place due to these various easements. We read many, many easement agreements to determine whether we could live with the restrictions. None of them were feasible because of restrictions not meeting the principles, values, and purpose of our family.

Multigenerational Living

With a seventh-generation philosophy in mind, they failed on many fronts.

For a successful outcome, base it on the preparation you have already accomplished as a family. You will find it much easier to reject many properties, by the process of elimination, that don't meet your specific criteria. It'll be painful at times. You will receive support from other family members during those difficult days, and sometimes you will support others. I've personally been involved in eight real estate transactions and have helped clients through hundreds of other transactions. Our transaction, by far, was the most difficult. It is a story unto itself that tested every one of us and was due to a number of bad actors. Maybe the pandemic had something to do with it?

* * *

Once you have your timeline and search parameters set, you are ready to begin the next stage, the transaction. Let's look at Stage 3, which deals with estate transactions.

STAGE THREE

The Multigenerational Living Estate Transaction

14

Setting Expectations

Many years ago, one of my mentors used to joke about how to prepare for a vacation. His comment, with a little bit of mirth in his manner, was, "Bring twice the money and half the clothes, and maybe you'll have enough money." My experience over time has mimicked this.

Your journey has now entered the transaction stage. Actually, it is much more of a transformation. Your life and that of your family members joining you on this journey will surely be transformed. Most everything you believe to be normal about living during our post-industrial modern era is going to be turned on its head.

In a way, your journey to living multi-generationally on your estate is one of the caveats of Charles Dickens' book, *Great Expectations*. As Pip grows into an adult, he experiences how society places value on social status, wealth, and position in life. We can draw many parallels to living as a family in modern American society. You are now on a journey to living multi-generationally and not being defined by your wealth or your position in society, which Charles Dickens would applaud. You will now be defined by how you live within your family community rather than a separate family unit.

Setting the Family Expectations

What is your family's expectation of the transformation you are about to make? This is a transformation from your nuclear family, where you manage your money, time, relationship, and purpose, to sharing these important freedoms with a broader set of related families.

One of the first eye-opening concepts I learned through Strategic Coach was how entrepreneurs are in the minority of individuals within the workforce who have complete freedom around their time, money, relationships, and purpose (The Four Freedoms®).[6] Most employees, including high-level executives, do not have these freedoms. Living multi-generationally on your family property certainly opens up freedom of purpose, arguably the most important freedom of The Four Freedoms. It may also broaden the freedom of relationships, expand your freedom of time through the support of other family members on the multigenerational living estate, and possibly provide more experiences that typically would be "bought" using disposable income afforded by freedom of money.

You felt the first real inklings of these freedoms when you developed a deeper sense of trusted communication, viable conflict resolution, collaborative visioning, and agreed-upon governance. When a family goes through the process of communication, conflict resolution, visioning, and then governance, they have spent about eight to ten full days or more going through that stage. That is why it feels different. This is different. It looks different, too, because the families have actually signed a governance document about how their family operated and how they will operate going forward. Some are being included for the first time in their life in major family decisions that once were decided by others.

There are, however, more people to agree upon a variety of decisions through consensus. It's more difficult to live when more people are involved. These expectations need to be addressed, as well as what The Four Freedoms look like for everyone on the estate.

What Is Your Greatest Expectation?

Buying a forever property is nothing like your last real estate purchase. You look at, feel, sense, smell, and taste the depth and breadth of this transaction—no, not transaction, but transformation. You will not look at the bricks and mortar or land the way you looked at it and felt about your current property. There is a permanence about this new place that will be in your family for seven generations. What is usually considered an expense is now considered an investment—an investment in future generations.

Perhaps you've heard this adage: *When is the best time to plant a tree? 20 years ago. When is the second best time to plant a tree? Today.* Why do I bring this up? Because you and your family are planting trees. There is a saying on my wall carved into wood that reminds me of how I treat our estate. "A society grows great when men plant trees whose shade they know they shall never sit in."

Every family member will feel a deep sense of purpose with one another. You all will have a sense of belonging and expectation. You must communicate your individual expectations at this time, especially those important thoughts and feelings tied up in your view of what living will be like on your multigenerational estate. All the preparation is complete. It is go time. Is everyone's go bag packed for this new journey?

Managing Expectations

We judge our experiences in life by our expectations, which are always present in every new encounter. This is a big one. Before your family begins your forever property search, discover whether everyone shared their individual expectation of that search. You'll be surprised by many of those expectations.

Once this communication is complete, then you may, as a collective group, set your family expectations of searching and purchasing your multigenerational property. Searching, completing the actual transaction, and then moving into your property can happen in as little as sixty days or take up to three years. Our search and closing took four months from when we began searching in earnest. We were fortunate, but you need to collectively set realistic expectations.

A longer time frame may be due to building your multigenerational living estate on raw land or rehabbing an existing property. If you haven't done so, determine whether your family is open to constructing or prefers buying an existing property so that no one is expecting a shorter time frame.

* * *

The first critical part of your search is meant to calm the emotional nature of searching out and selecting a new home, especially a forever home. Once everyone agrees on the expectations for the time frame and other related issues, you may then move on to mapping out the area where you will apply your search parameters.

15

Location

If you hail from Wisconsin, you know how difficult it is for a "cheesehead" to move to that state south of the Wisconsin border—Illinois. For many, it's a repugnant thought to join those "flatlanders." The same goes for many lifelong Illinoisans when they consider moving north to join the Packer-crazed fans when they know the entire history of George Halas and the Monsters of the Midway, the Chicago Bears. Similarly, New York Yankee fans would not be caught dead in a Boston Red Sox jersey or vice versa.

Where Will You Live?

Besides regional biases, your family may have required geographical features. Without the features that specifically support the families' interests, the property is a non-starter. Your family may long for mountains, oceans, deserts, lakes, rivers, plains, or a mix of geographical environments to meet the collective desires and wants of family members.

Our family was specific in this area due to our visceral ties to the land to fulfill familial hunting traditions. Several of our families participate in the sport of Orienteering. Orienteers are an interesting breed. You must be a little bit "touched" to love running in the woods while carefully reading a topographical map and navigating to purposefully placed markers on a variety of geographical features. We love the forests, rivers, lakes, streams, mountains, and fields.

Therefore, most of these elements had to be present in our property, which is a tall order in many parts of the country.

Your family may want to have ready access to a particular metropolitan area, possibly making the process of finding that ideal property challenging. The non-negotiable requirements of the geographical makeup of your land may be a hard standard to fulfill. You may have land features that are non-negotiables that will eliminate many properties.

Location is important to consider when you run a business that requires extensive travel. A major airport must be within a reasonable travel distance otherwise, the property is unsuitable. How far are you and your family willing to travel from a major airport? How far from healthcare services? How far from quality schools?

With young children living on your multigenerational living estate, the local public or private schools, along with demographics, activities, cultural biases, and more, come into play. If your property is located in an unacceptable school district, then private schools or homeschooling may be the only acceptable choices. In some areas of the country, school choices are limited. Will you send your children to boarding school? Will you set up your own homeschooling curriculum? You could become part of a private school. One group of entrepreneurs actually structured and built a private school due to the inadequate educational facilities in their region. Their children are now part of a school that emphasizes both indoor and outdoor hands-on education.

Where will you grocery or retail shop? Where will you play golf and tennis, boat, fish, hunt, or ride horses? How about restaurants, forest preserves, community activities, social and civic clubs? Think of all the activities you and your family enjoy, and then consider where you will find them or whether your estate will provide them.

Location, Location, Location

You are now aware that what you've grown accustomed to as normal is being replaced with a new normal when you choose to live on a multigenerational estate. Your extraordinary estate will change your lifestyle in ways you still can't predict. You and your families are taking a risk, a leap of faith. You'll feel fulfilled by some aspects but will find many challenges requiring workarounds.

To find our dream property, we took a map of West Virginia, Virginia, Maryland, and Pennsylvania and drew an outline of our target area. There were geographical limitations due to family members' work-related travel requirements, although less so due to the new COVID-driven work and home schedules at the time. We drove around our chosen area many times, researching all the elements that affected our core estate non-negotiables as part of our principles, purpose, and vision statement.

We then drew a roughly one-hundred-by-thirty-mile area covering portions of the four states (West Virginia, Virginia, Maryland, and Pennsylvania) even though we were prejudiced about living in either West Virginia or Maryland, primarily because many family members had lived for decades in southeast and northern Virginia. The minimum acceptable acreage was twenty acres with a somewhat equal mix of forest and fields with elevation relief for agriculture and hunting opportunities. More acreage was acceptable, but in this area of the country little acreage larger than about one hundred acres would meet our other non-negotiable criteria.

Have you decided on your land composition, location, must-haves, and non-starters? I mentioned this earlier, but do so again to stress its importance: What do you do now on a daily basis? You have routines that are not easily erased. Dig deep and write down, in detail, how you live and what you do. Do you exercise indoors or outdoors, and will that change after the move? Do you eat out regularly? Are you used to shopping on a daily basis? Your multigenerational estate's location may double or more the time that it takes you presently to go shopping, stop at a coffee shop, take yoga classes, swim in a public pool, and so on. Are you used to pitch-black nights with limited noise pollution? This can be unnerving if you've not experienced it night after night.

One of the families we interviewed had to change their daily shopping routine to once weekly because their property was now thirty minutes from all the places they needed to visit. After two years of living on their estate, they are still adjusting.

If two, three, or more of your simple daily routines are non-negotiables, then your multigenerational estate must provide this capability. It is difficult to adjust, rebuild, or reconfigure the buildings or grounds after you've moved in. Maybe you and your family members need to live on a property similar to what you are searching for to determine what is not acceptable. The last thing you want to hear from a close family member after moving in is, "I can't live here. I'm done."

Reaching Consensus Before Moving In

Once again, I stress the importance of communication and consensus. It is unlikely that every family member will love every aspect of your estate. That would be perfection. Expect some give-and-take. Everyone will sacrifice something they currently take for granted and may believe they can't live without it. Are you willing to accept an 80 percent result for your negotiables? Does every family member buy into the entire multigenerational living situation, focusing on the overall result and not one particular area? Have you ever lived on a property in a location that had everything you needed and wanted where most, if not all, of your properties met your needs? If not, your time there was probably limited.

Your multigenerational living estate can't miss any of the needs of any family member; otherwise, it will just be a matter of time before they leave the property.

* * *

A few chapters ago, we touched on search parameters but not at the level and depth necessary to move forward. Chapter 16 will delve more deeply into those parameters to help guide the search for your right-fit property.

16

Search Parameters

Searching through the multiple listing service (MLS), Zillow, or other real estate-related software for a potential new home is commonplace today. Searching for a potential multigenerational living estate is quite a different story. Even though a plethora of information is available online, proper due diligence during and after a multigenerational living property visit will uncover much more.

We viewed these properties through a three-generation lens with a seventh-generation philosophical approach. On one of our visits, the next generation mentioned that we would be "leaving the property in a pine box." The finality of this statement is stark and puts into context what sort of undertaking you are pursuing.

Zoning and Easements

Zoning is probably the most difficult area to research and understand. You'll quickly learn that larger properties may have easements placed on them—historical, environmental, charitable, municipal, federal, state, utility, and so on. In the 1980s and 1990s, due to the hefty estate tax burden, estate planners were pushing heavily to place easements on large high-end properties to lessen the estate taxes upon the owner's death. These easements, by and large, are permanent.

Many potential properties that met all our non-negotiables did not pass our flexibility standard. We couldn't easily determine how our family could utilize a property in the future. We did know that an easement might limit the construction of new infrastructure and building usage. We discovered that the restrictive language addressing many factors sometimes requires approval by strangers who are ill-equipped to make these choices about our family's desire to fulfill our vision and purpose.

The property of one of the multigenerational estate owners we interviewed backs up to federal land that is part of an established federal park. In the past, bad actors had taken advantage of the remoteness of this land through illegal logging, hunting, and other illegal activities. So, the family has worked with numerous offices and dozens of federal employees over the decades. Sometimes, the employees were cooperative, at times hostile, and other times, humble enough to understand and take advice from the family on how to protect and preserve the land. It is in the best interest of the government and the family to have a healthy relationship due to the integrative geography that affects both parties.

The learning point here is understanding your land and the land adjacent to your property. It is not unusual for families to want to purchase adjacent properties to protect the land, manage the forest, provide regenerative techniques to improve farm fields and protect the local watershed. Know what easements are adjacent to your property and conduct your due diligence. After a short period of time on your estate, you will learn how very important the responsibilities of being a prudent caretaker of the land can be.

Some easements are long-term leases of one hundred years that then revert to ownership by the county, state, historical, or charitable organizations. If this were simply another home in the history of homes you have owned, then a lease coming due in seventy or eighty years is someone else's issue. Not so on a well-established multigenerational estate. Some easements specify roadways, square footage, height, length, and depth of buildings with aggregate limitations. Many easements run over thirty pages in length, referring to other documents on file with families who placed these easements, even requiring approval from the heirs of former estate owners. It can get very complicated, very messy, and downright depressing. We encountered three separate properties that fit all our requirements just to have the easements take enough away that we decided to walk away.

Housing Requirements

Property features (bedrooms, baths, fireplaces, basements, etc.) are usually at the top of the list of needs or must-haves when searching for single-family residences. If the "bones" of the property are in good shape, then rehabbing, additions, or other construction can remedy many of the interior features.

However, with multiple families living on a property, more emphasis is placed on the separation of families geographically within the multigenerational estate. Making the transition from your nuclear family to multigenerational living is a big move, and many families want to maintain the separation they are accustomed to with their nuclear family. This desire makes the physical location of each "single family property" on the multigenerational property an important consideration. Your property may require you to construct new residences to accommodate the number of families moving onto the estate. Your property may require enough space to allow for gardens, a pool, a pickleball court, a separate office workspace environment, and land large enough to accommodate chickens, sheep, goats, cows, or other animals. You may need to carve out roadways and land improvements for proper drainage or recreational activities.

To put this in context, we started by establishing a little over 120 projects on our multigenerational living property. Some were completed within a year, while others will take ten to twenty years or more. There are always multiple projects at various stages of development going on. The forest, in particular, started to grow and develop in the late 1950s when a large man-made reservoir was established along a nearby riverbed. This forest is now mature, so one of our projects is to prudently manage it.

Inspect the Properties

Each property is unique. Due to topography, architecture, age, and upkeep of properties, they have unique qualities with unique challenges and unique opportunities. Your search parameters will get you only so far. Your property visits round out the intangibles that search parameters can't easily address.

These multigenerational living estate visits take the better part of a day. You may be able to accomplish two visits in a day, but that would be a very long and exhausting day. Besides walking through the buildings (one property we visited had over twenty buildings), you will want to discover and vet the all-important surrounding acreage on the property. How close is the property to a major highway or busy road? What level of noise pollution is present?

Light pollution? Water pollution? Are the exterior utilities (septic, well, propane, fuel park, etc.) appropriate, efficient, and up to code? Where is the nearest medical facility? Extreme rural environments are non-starters for access to healthcare for elder generations.

Be sure to invite and involve family members and their unique abilities on these visits. Does someone have electrical expertise and could inspect the wires and fuse boxes? Who has a good sense of spacing and could specifically look at the interior layout for it being a fit for your family? What about the landscape and gardening potentials? Make sure you have family members who can look at specifics on the properties that go with you. This will save you time and money if you can eliminate properties with identifiable flaws upfront before the inspection stage uncovers thousands of dollars of repairs that need to be completed prior to completing the sale.

Services and Utilities

A big consideration with rural properties is a high-speed internet connection. This may become less important with services like Starlink (high-speed internet via satellite) coming online recently. We considered building on one property and estimated wiring for the internet would cost $250,000. Even with high-speed internet available at our main house on our current property, we had to rewire and connect multiple buildings at a substantial cost.

Multigenerational Living

Rural living has challenges such as standalone utilities, a safe water supply, and nearby business activities. We are fortunate, on the one hand, to have heavy restrictions on business operations on nearby local premises, but also hamstrung by not being able to host a variety of paid events such as weddings, concerts, or wine-tasting rooms. Fortunately, we are not planning on these activities presently. However, our future generations may find these particular regulations too onerous to live by.

There's a fine line between being so rural that land and housing are inexpensive but access to amenities is scarce and difficult versus living on the outskirts of collar suburbs where more infrastructure is available but regulations are greater.

* * *

It would be impossible to cover all the parameters that you may require. You'll be more precise and have a better gut feeling about a property once you have visited a few within your price range. After seeing some of these properties, the real work begins: determining which property to make an offer on. Your family members will have their preferences, so how can you make the right selection? Here is when the questions can mount up so quickly that you may freeze and be filled with anxiety. The following chapter will help you use communication and consensus to work through those issues of having too many choices, that is, overchoice.

17

Overchoice

Consider that the average grocery store has forty-five thousand items while Walmart carries up to one hundred thousand items. You probably buy the same brand of bread or olive oil or laundry detergent every time you visit the grocery store. If you didn't, you would experience the common everyday issue of overchoice.

In 2010, Sheena S. Iyengar wrote the bestselling book *The Art of Choosing*. She's an expert on the subject of overchoice, which we face every day. In a 2012 TEDx Talk, she walked through four simple techniques to mitigate choice overload: less is more (cut choices), consequences need to be felt in a concrete way, categorization, and condition of complexity. Let's look at how her techniques apply to your search for the right-fit multigenerational property.

Less Is More

Your family has documented the non-negotiables that must be present in a property. We had six in total. As

Sheena would comment, less is more. If you have more than twenty non-negotiables, that may make the decision process more difficult, and you may want to work with your family to pare down your list. One of Sheena's studies involved a jam taste test at a grocery store. One group tested six brands of jam, while the other group taste-tested twenty-four brands. As it turned out, those who tested the six brands were six times more likely to buy jam.[7] So, your first technique is to keep your non-negotiables down to a manageable number.

Progress, not perfection, is my rule. I often must remind myself that in an imperfect world, progress is my only results-based measuring stick. Perfection exists in places like the classroom, where you may score 100 percent on an exam. The real world is messy. One best-selling author I know with over twenty published books accepts a 30 percent result on a first draft of a new book he is writing. Life is messy. Measure only your progress.

Concretely Felt Consequences

Reading online about the beautiful property you're about to visit with a focus on the most ideal circumstances and viewing phenomenal pictures under perfect weather conditions is not concrete. But those eloquent paragraphs and gorgeous photos won't portray reality. Visit the property on a rainy day. Visit it after dark. Make a surprise visit, with limited notice, before making an offer. See all the messes and imperfections. Compare your impression with those of your family members before selecting that property.

Always hold a meeting with your family members immediately after visiting a potential property. Even if you know the property is not the right fit, you'll experience and learn something new that you can apply to other property visits. What you learned, no matter its appropriateness, will make the next visit that much more useful. Capture the learning while it is fresh, visceral, and vivid in your mind to help in the process of selecting your right-fit property.

Categorize Your Non-negotiables

Categorization is important with multigenerational living estate visits. Your non-negotiables help categorize the properties to visit. Unlike viewing single-family homes, which may allow for four or more visits in a day, a multigenerational property is a whole-day affair. Your non-negotiables will eliminate the vast majority of properties if one of your non-negotiables is not present on the property.

Maintaining a rhythm and flow to the search process is all-important. The search is a marathon and not a sprint. You may only be able to view two properties weekly while doing online searches and preparing for visits takes up your time the rest of the week. Some family members may not be available for every visit but may tag along if you use video and audio while visiting a prospective property.

Complexity

Sheena's last, simple technique to avoid overchoice is the condition of complexity. Her real-world study mentioned above showed that starting with the easiest choices (in our case, fewer) to the hardest choices (many) was most effective in completing your due diligence on a property. For your multigenerational estate search parameters, the easiest choices are your non-negotiables. We had six of those and about fifteen negotiables. Don't start with the negotiables. They won't matter unless all of the non-negotiables are present.

Communication Matters

During the search process, some family members will become overwhelmed. Communicate, communicate, and communicate. The complexity and number of factors to consider is exponentially greater than with a single-family property. There is a possibility of complete overload and brain exhaustion. Continual communication helps to keep stress in check and gives everyone permission to back off when the going gets too rough for them. Communicate daily to keep everyone moving in the same direction.

Visit Other Multigenerational Living Estates

Visit existing multigenerational estates. Talk to their families. Find out all the wonderful experiences and see all the warts and shortcomings. You'll learn many things from their experiences that you can apply to your situation. We have been on over a dozen visits. Without fail, we learn something new every single time.

Cutting Down the Choices

The key to narrowing down your choices to one property you will make an offer on is going through the process of elimination. Your non-negotiables will provide the best, fastest, and easiest way to accomplish this seemingly Herculean task. The other factor is the overall gut feeling or emotion you have about a property. Studies have shown that our gut brain is more intuitive when it comes to the intangible, hard-to-make decisions in life. We did not move forward seriously on any property unless our key four family members unanimously agreed on the right fit of a particular property.

* * *

Trust me, eventually, you'll land on that right-fit property. And when you do, it will be time to make an offer. In the next chapter, we'll explore all the elements you'll need to ensure you've created a good, solid offer.

18

The Contract

In 1985, I attended a No Money Down two-day real estate conference put on by Robert G. Allen, along with a thousand other attendees. At the time, he was considered the expert at buying properties with no down payment, a very appealing proposition. Shortly thereafter, I obtained my real estate license to ensure I understood all aspects of real estate, especially the real estate contract. Robert G. Allen gave the impression that real estate contracts generally favor the seller. We were on a quest to write buyers contracts that supposedly would be full of legal (weasel) clauses allowing us to get out of the contract without any negative repercussions.

The lesson from this short stint into real estate investing was to provide as much flexibility as possible on any potential investment real estate transaction with no money down. That's laughable now after I've been involved in eight transactions and assisted my clients in hundreds of other transactions.

Multigenerational living properties are legal beasts. Any seller of a large multiple-building, multi-use property knows the time frame is stretched out much longer than in a single-family home transaction. The property's marketing is unique, the listing is more complex, and the financing can be a nightmare. Multigenerational living property sellers expect that the buyer will have difficulty with two areas in particular: property inspection and financing.

The Purchase Contract

Generally, three areas are expertly reviewed when writing a multigenerational-living real estate purchase contract: inspection, financing, and easements. Contracts have many more parts, but these three tend to be the most difficult compared to your experience purchasing a single-family residence. The contract will be written to allow for these three contingencies to be in place over a certain period of time or based on other factors (for example, interest rate ceiling for financing, irreparable structural issues, etc.).

Multi-building properties may take days or even weeks to inspect. We had a crew of four inspectors spend an entire day on one of our residential buildings. The checklist of deficiencies was twenty pages long. Thankfully, none were critical. The bones of the 13,000-square-foot building were solid. Then, they had five more buildings to go.

Rural properties require well and septic inspections in addition to building inspections. For many financial underwriters, these items must meet the appropriate state and local standards to pass inspection. In addition, the well and septic may not meet your standards based on how many family members will occupy the property. We had to put in an additional well (making four in total) to ensure the appropriate reservoir and flow rate could sustain five families.

Back to your real estate contract. Unlike the typical sixty-day window to close, you will most likely need

90–180 days in order to complete the due diligence and sign off on all the contingencies on your selected property. The seller's agent and counsel recognize the difficulty in completing these larger transactions but will still negotiate for a shorter window of time to complete the transaction. Not to worry; this is typical, and everyone involved expects unforeseen delays to impact closing on time.

Financing Your Property

Financing a personal real estate property falls into conventional, non-conventional, and private mortgages. Conventional loans have the typical 20 percent down payment with a thirty-year fixed or adjustable rate mortgage. These loans are conforming or non-conforming (jumbo). If your property qualifies for conventional underwriting, the loan will most likely be a jumbo, non-conforming loan.

Alternatives to conventional loans are FHA and VA loans (offered to veterans). These loans have slightly stricter underwriting requirements and typically allow for much lower or no down payment. There is typically a limit on the maximum dollar amount allowed to underwrite these non-conventional mortgages. Conventional mortgages have limits as well. Therefore, these financing options may not be available for your property.

Finally, private investors and investment groups will make loans available to multigenerational property owners. Their terms are generally twenty-year amortized loans with some kind of adjustable rate five years into the term of the loan. These loans look more like conventional commercial property loans. They may run 1 percent to 5 percent higher than the prevailing rates for conventional and non-conventional loans.

It's possible that neither conventional nor non-conventional loans will be available due to the strict underlying guidelines on these mortgages. For instance, any income generated by the property immediately disqualifies that property for these loans. Also, these loans may not be available should your property have multiple structures or the acreage exceeds a certain limit. There may be circumstances that allow for underwriting, but it's highly unlikely.

When purchasing undeveloped land, the down payment may be closer to 30 percent of the land purchase price. Conventional and non-conventional construction loans for conversion upon completion of multiple residences and outbuildings may not be available. Private investment loans may be the only choice for financing to complete the new construction on the property.

If your family is forming an LLC or other legal entity to purchase a property, then conventional and non-conventional underwriting will not be available. These legal entities may be required to gather the down payment and support whatever financing is available by multiple family members buying the property under a homeowner's association (HOA) agreement. Conventional and non-conventional underwriting requires a lien directly against an individual or individuals; otherwise, financing is not available.

That leaves private investing as your primary funding choice. Before covering this area, be aware other government funding agencies are available for family farms or other specialized types of properties. It will pay dividends to research available funding sources for your particular property.

Private investment or investment groups typically look for a higher rate of return than what they can receive from the public markets. Therefore, the interest rates they offer often are 1 percent to 5 percent higher than current traditional mortgage rates. The higher rate is due to the investment pool being offered for fewer loans than the massive loan packages sold off in the public markets, which are funded by the conventional and non-conventional loans of millions of residential properties.

How do you find a private lender? Private lender groups make their products available through traditional independent mortgage origination companies. This area of funding has been growing rapidly over the past decade due to more restrictions being placed on traditional mortgage underwriting. It only takes one box to be checked off incorrectly to be denied a loan, even though the buyer may have an excellent credit score and liquid assets that could pay off the mortgage many times over. Yes, it has gotten that bad.

Contingencies

The contingency for financing is a critical part of your real estate contract offer primarily because it may take up to ninety days or more to secure financing. It is not unusual to pick a date for closing only to have to push it back multiple times while waiting for approval and then waiting to be provided the funds for closing. While securing financing, the all-important PITI (principal, interest, taxes, and insurance) must be monitored to ensure you do not go over budget. Adding an appropriate ceiling on the interest rate to the real estate contract is critical to allow you to back out if financing becomes too onerous.

Lastly, we must consider the contingencies for easements. Many easements do not surface until after the title search takes place, so your contract must include a contingency to accommodate these unwelcome surprises, as well as a contingency for underwriting the known easements. You'll want to hire a local real estate attorney to research all the easements on your selected property.

The lender may require a new survey of your multi-generational estate. When purchasing a larger property, it is not unusual to discover that your potential property violates boundary markers with roadways, fences, or other easements. You may need to rectify these issues before closing or waive them, if allowed, by the mortgage underwriter.

Due to its unique aspects, each property will have particular contingencies placed in the contract. This is why having a knowledgeable real estate agent is important. They will have the local experience and expertise on how to deal with issues exclusive to the area. It may take the better part of a day to walk the property again and note any substantive matters. If not addressed in the contract, you may inherit unwelcome and unwanted problems with the property purchase.

Sigh. This entire chapter can be downright depressing. You may feel that I'm constantly dumping cold water on the state and future of your multigenerational living estate. Legal contracts and all that goes into them are intentionally difficult to read, and it's a challenge to not allow yourself to be overwhelmed. Contract law has its place, and it protects the seller and the buyer based on our strong rule of law.

* * *

The following chapter addresses the all-important task of constant, consistent, and positive communication, which will keep your family bonds strong. This time frame between making the offer to the closing is an emotional rollercoaster and one of the most difficult times of preparing to live multi-generationally on your family's new estate.

19

Multigenerational Living Estate Transaction Meetings

A popular book came out in 1992 by author Gary Chapman titled *The Five Love Languages*. His premise is that each of us has a desire to be loved in one of five particular manners: words of affirmation, quality time, physical touch, acts of service, and receiving gifts. I'm not certain which one fits my wife; however, what I'm certain of is being in constant communication with her. Staying in touch with her has kept our relationship strong and vibrant over forty-plus years of marriage.

Communicate Regularly with Your Family Members

Communication is the most important element of living with many family members on your estate. It needs to be constant, consistent, and clear. Those earlier sessions of building trusted communication and conflict resolution will pay dividends when you are wondering what you just got yourself involved in.

Real estate transactions are stressful, even more so for a complex, multi-faceted, multigenerational living estate transaction. Every day, deadlines need attention to keep the transaction on track. What starts out as a fairly straightforward process can quickly run into roadblocks and detours. Communication among and between family members is paramount to seeing the transaction through successfully.

The financial underwriting alone can be complicated, especially if the contract is submitted by a family entity (LLC or other entity) involving multiple family members. The underwriters will require all family members to submit credit scores and tax returns and complete financial statements. They will require cross-collateralization, meaning each family may end up being entirely responsible for the entire lien on the property. Those family members with deeper pockets will have the most, at least monetarily, to lose.

If you haven't discussed individual family personal finances before the underwriting began, now is the time to do so. Americans have a phobia around money and finances. Studies have discovered that we are twice as likely to discuss sexual preferences, drug and alcohol abuse, and political leanings as we are to discuss our salary or what we've saved for retirement. You will need to have some frank and difficult discussions around money and joint family finances.

We talked earlier about how overwhelming inspections of large properties can be. The report may be the size of a medium-length book that reviews the many checklists of infrastructure, mechanicals, electrical, HVAC, and general condition of the property. The meeting after receiving the inspection report can be intense. Why? Because a group of professionals is going to rain all over your parade. They will

Multigenerational Living

expose all the good, the bad, and the ugly of your future multigenerational living estate. Remember, you are buying a small town. Everything is multiplied by three, five, or ten times the normal single-family home inspection. The inspection meeting determines whether your family can live with the probable time, money, and frustration of correcting property deficiencies over time.

Our property had over $1 million of repairs, additions, and replacements to make in order to get it to where we wanted it to be. This took several years. We understood from the beginning that this might be the case because the property had been unoccupied for over two years. The bones, or infrastructure, were in good order, so no major changes were required in an area that could be very expensive. Our property was sold as is, but we spent over $40,000 in repairs on it before closing. This allowed us to obtain financing based on deficiencies that needed to be corrected based on the property's appraisal. Afterward, though, simply replacing the necessary electrical outlets and faceplates has cost over $5,000.

We met three times weekly during the stressful closing period. While our closing was relatively quick, taking just over nine weeks of underwriting, we encountered obstacles almost every day, including bad actors who caused additional stress, anxiety, and frustration. One bad actor was the underwriter, who lied to us and was not prepared for our closing, delaying it by a week. The underwriter didn't believe it was possible to complete mold mitigation in two buildings, including inspections before and after mitigation. We completed this remediation with the help of dedicated professionals over a Friday, Saturday, and Sunday. Additionally, we personally spent days on the property making corrections to various deficiencies (replacing HVAC systems, safety installations, etc.). Our experience is not that unusual as I have come to find out from others who had similar experiences. They all cautioned us to be prepared for the long haul.

You and your family will have to tackle issue after issue until everything is completed for closing. Constant, consistent communication is a key element in maintaining your sanity. You may have to dig deep as a family to see one another through some difficult experiences. This pre-closing experience is an excellent primer for what is to come after you move onto the property. We continued to deal with many surprises during the first year on our property.

Dealing with Surveys, Appraisals, and Sellers

Surveys and appraisals may be difficult as well. As we've seen with inspections, a survey can take the better part of a day or two days. Then, property disputes may come up as a result of the survey, which may need to be rectified before closing. These disputes can delay closing by many months as you wait for the property titles to clear.

Appraisals are a whole other story unto themselves. With the passage of the laws to protect consumers after the great financial crisis of 2007–2008, the Dodd-Frank Wall Street Reform and Consumer Protection Act of 2010 put in place requirements for unbiased appraisals. Prior to that legislation, you had some control over selecting an appraiser known for experience and competency. Currently, selecting the appraiser is completely random. You may have a good, mediocre, or an inadequate appraiser. We were fortunate to have a thirty-year veteran appraiser who was extremely helpful in performing the appraisal and also providing several professionals to fix the problems that surfaced through the appraisal.

The final area that can be emotionally charged is dealing with the seller and their particular idiosyncrasies about the property they are selling. They may not want to fix any existing problems with the property. Many properties are sold "as is" due to the plethora of possible issues to address. The owner of our property was a foreign entity. We had to communicate through their US-based attorneys, then through Canadian attorneys, and then to the foreign country legal counsel. It took a week to get approval on any change to the contract. Fortunately, we were not dealing with a seller's possible emotional reactions. They wanted the property off their books. You may not be as fortunate.

Real estate transactions are personal, and opinions run the gamut. Feelings are hurt even when no malice is meant. Sellers and buyers can get sideways very quickly. If you don't have a strong mediator in your family who's involved in this transaction, you may need to seek counsel to help keep everything on track. In the heat of a real estate transaction, we can become unreasonable very quickly. Keep on communicating—constantly and consistently—as the process moves along. Address all misgivings, misunderstandings, and legitimate or misplaced feelings as soon as they arise.

* * *

At times, you will wonder why you agreed to purchase your multigenerational living estate. The transaction may push your family to the brink. It will be a great test to determine how well family members deal with money, stress, and emotional turmoil.

At long last, you'll close on your multigenerational property, and you'll want to celebrate. Remember to celebrate your wins. They will happen periodically on your multigenerational estate. Have some fun and relish the accomplishment. Enjoy the first day of owning your property. Breathe in, breathe out, because now, the real work begins.

STAGE FOUR
The Estate Transformation

20

Day One, A Learning, or Winning, Mindset

Americans love their sports franchises. Having lived in the Midwest for many years, there is nothing like the emotional highs and lows a fan of the Chicago Bears, Green Bay Packers, or Cleveland Browns (Are there any Browns fans left?) feel. It's all about winning. It's a binary thing. There are the winners, and there are the losers. This is how the game is played. This winning mindset is so prevalent in our culture that even mentioning a winning or learning mindset seems heretical. Earning A's in school and being on a winning basketball team doesn't represent life after graduation. Neither is winning or losing. What's true in life is some things work, and some things don't work. Sometimes you succeed and when you don't, you'll have learned from the experience.

Entrepreneurs know this all too well. They are used to many, many failures. Peter Diamandis, best known for his XPRIZE® competition, is fond of saying: "The day before something is truly a breakthrough, it's a crazy idea."[8] What goes through the mind of an entrepreneur and how they live day-to-day is based on a learning, or winning, mindset. Multigenerational living is like that on a daily basis. You are breaking new ground. Your family will go to places they have not experienced before. Many decisions and actions will fail. Your family will learn from these changes and failures.

This is not what most people experience on a daily basis. Having a learning mindset helps set the mental table to accept the fact that we know very little about living multi-generationally. We lost that "institutional" knowledge generations ago when we left rural life for the new industrial jobs in urban environments. Social psychologists recognize that we learn through doing and through the experience of our failures and successes.

Adopt a Learning Mindset to Win

One of my primary reasons for writing this book was to help you avoid those big failures and mistakes that could seriously jeopardize your new lifestyle. As neophytes in this world of multigenerational living, our innocence and lack of knowledge can be disconcerting as we fail more often than we did when living with our nuclear family. Be open to getting most of it wrong the first time.

How about first accepting this truism? With this totally new experience, without the aid of an instruction manual or mentor to direct you toward a better outcome, you will fail. And that is okay. Failures are how we learn, but they are not fun experiences. Remember when we talked about progress, not perfection? Our goal is for this phase of learning to live multi-generationally to *not* be catastrophic. Quick, continuous failing, failing forward, and learning from failure is the name of this new game.

With this mindset in every experience, you'll have only one of two possible outcomes: learning or winning. In the entrepreneurial world, learning is *not* receiving the order or the check, and winning *is* receiving the order and the check. It's a results-based approach, and living multi-generationally is a results-based approach. The word *because*, often used in authoritarian-run nuclear families, doesn't work in this environment. You must practice and learn trusted communication and conflict resolution to effectively live in harmony with your newfound "extended" family.

Next Steps and New Ideas

As they become accustomed to the multigenerational living environment, family members will want to stretch their wings and start to fly. They will want to enter into new ventures, hobbies, and activities that require time, resources, effort, and money. Money is usually the determinant that defines the learning or the winning outcome.

One of the lessons I heard from marketing guru Dean Jackson is the technique Jim Collins created called bullets to cannonballs. I'm paraphrasing here. When marketing a new idea, it is best to start small, say with one thousand prospects and $1,000, to determine if your marketing idea will yield positive results. After testing and annotating the results, adjust the marketing to go out again to one thousand new prospects, spending $1,000. This may occur several times until you've honed in on the sweet spot. Now, you can take out your cannon and blast fifty thousand prospects for $50,000.

This technique recognizes that your idea may or may not be feasible. Test first with a small amount of money. Learn from the results and then test again. Money is a limited resource. On a multigenerational living estate, operating expenses can run high, and money can be stretched thinly. New ideas, prospects, activities, and hobbies need to be tested before spending significant time, effort, resources, and money.

The key is to establish a learning and winning mindset before embarking on a new venture. It may be that the particular project is not worth the time, effort, resources, and money for the return expected. Not every new initiative is about tangible results. Some lead to new experiences that fulfill an individual's purpose or a collective family purpose. Stress, anxiety, and frustration can arise when good money chases after bad as a particular initiative continues to flounder and fail.

Habits and Mindsets

The learning and winning mindset applies to habits as well. Forming a new habit is difficult. Many attempts will be made to live life differently on your multigenerational living estate. Over time, those differences will show up in new habits that replace current habits. As adults, we generally do not add to our current set of habits. Habits are deeply-rooted ways we seamlessly operate. They are the "fast" thinking that Daniel Kahneman mentions in his popular tome, *Thinking Fast and Slow*.[9] Habits require two full years to "know" something newly learned.

What does knowing a habit mean? Many books talk about forming new habits. Most state that a habit takes between fourteen and twenty-one days to be established. An established habit is not the same as a deeply subconscious-level knowing habit. That is why health clubs have a rise in membership each January, only to see a few new daily users by April. The majority of those established habits never make it to the "knowing" level.

Multigenerational Living

Establishing a habit is somewhat of a surface habit initially. It lives in your conscious mind. It requires tremendous willpower, and we have only a limited supply of willpower to use daily. To know a habit is to subconsciously and automatically perform that habit. Take the real-life example of learning to drive. Insurance company automobile rates for young people under the age of twenty-five are much higher than the general population. The explanation is simple. When a dangerous situation arises on the road, the inexperienced driver must consciously think about pressing down on the long skinny pedal (accelerator) or the fat wide one (brake). That split second of additional conscious processing time can be the difference between avoiding or not avoiding an accident. An experienced driver who knows how to drive is not even consciously aware of their action until after it is performed automatically by their powerfully quick subconscious mind. That is why younger people have more accidents, and the insurance companies rate their insurance premiums higher.

Living multi-generationally will generate many new habits for family members. Those habits will take two years to form and know and will necessitate lots of learning and less winning. Without the learning and winning mindset, the probability of success is reduced. We are back in school again, feeling awkward and unsure of our every action. Remember, that feeling comes with the territory. The good news is everyone will experience the same awkwardness, so we can all laugh together as we learn how to live and operate much differently than when we were sequestered in our individual families.

Each and every day, take stock of your current attitude, your outlook, and your demeanor. Determine whether you are learning and winning or are in failure mode. Failure mode can become the default for you and many of your other family members on your estate. It can completely take over, festering like a cancer that spreads to all parts of your life and the lives of those living on your property. Communicate your feelings with one another—you are all there to help one another succeed on your new estate.

* * *

We learned so much from their experiences through our interviews and visits with other multigenerational living families. In the following chapter, let's look at how you can take advantage of this knowledge. We don't need to make all the same mistakes. We can certainly learn from the mistakes of others.

21

Multigenerational Living Estate Visits

When our company goes through the process of interviewing and hiring a new team member, we look for and will only make an offer to those who possess four key core company principles. One of those principles is coachability. Coachable people are open to new learning; that is, they're open to considering they may be doing something incorrectly or learning how to improve their skills and abilities by taking direction from others.

Be the Empty Cup

There's a story of a Japanese Zen master who was asked to teach Zen to an accomplished professor. The Zen master was pouring tea into the professor's cup when suddenly the cup was overflowing. The professor could not contain himself and said, "It's overflowing. No more will go in!"

The Zen master stopped and replied, "Like the cup, you are too full of your own opinions and speculations. How can I show you Zen until you first empty your cup?"[10]

Living with the families on your estate is easier if you empty your cup of all your opinions and speculations about living this new lifestyle. You need to have a certain level of humility. We know very little about this new adventure—we are learning. We will get much of it wrong the first time. Of course, we would like to speed up the process to get there sooner rather than later. However, there is nothing noble about building every "wheel" from scratch. Many other families have formed their multigenerational living estates and have failed and learned from their mistakes. We can learn from their experiences.

Seeking out and searching for others who share the same experiences can be helpful. Every family approaches living multi-generationally on their property differently. Like many new experiences, you'll find others in your travels as you make new friends and meet other families through your colleagues and networks as they become aware of your new lifestyle.

There are family compounds, family farms, homesteads, and other ways of experiencing this lifestyle. Each family has unique skills and capabilities. They spend their time and effort to successfully accomplish different aspects of living this new exciting lifestyle. One family may be learning animal husbandry and applying it to sheep, pigs, goats, and cattle. Another may be developing regenerative farming techniques and practices while successfully growing vegetables, cover crops, flowers, and fruit trees. And yet another may have improved their property for outdoor activities such as trail riding, horseback lessons/training, pickleball and playing fields, special occasion venues, and more.

Multigenerational Living

We have been on at least a dozen multigenerational living estates, homesteads, or other related visits. We've learned something new each time, and many times, multiple new lessons in areas we were just starting to develop and test. More importantly, we learned the must-dos and don't-dos. We often heard from others on multigenerational properties, "If we had just known about A, B, or C going in, we would have saved a lot of time, effort, resources, and money." Money is the big one. Many families have wasted hundreds of thousands of dollars on projects, only to realize later the extent of their costly mistake. Pay attention, take direction, and do not repeat those mistakes.

Family homesteads often barely eke out a living. The families are learning to live off the bounty of the land with limited resources, land, and money. Their ingenuity and dogged determination to live independently of mainstream goods while raising families is awesome. Yet, weather, wild animals, disease, and insects seem to have a single-minded goal of destroying everything that is being grown or trying to kill and eat the animals being raised. We have taken these lessons to heart.

The more costly mistakes happen when major rehab or building takes place to host a variety of events, from special events to corporate outings, storage, office space, or business opportunities. One multigenerational living family spent a year of their time and a substantial amount of money to upgrade a 150-year-old barn as a venue. They held their first event and, as they expected, successfully made a nice profit. The following week, a county official showed up and shut down their venue. Apparently, a few years earlier, the county stopped the development of any new or future venues. A great loss could have been avoided had they first checked out any local restrictions or requirements. We are in the same county and were considering the same thing. Whew! That was one costly mistake we avoided.

Meet Your Neighbors

Estate visits are valuable. We have made new friends for life. One of the attributes of living rurally is the openness your neighbors extend to help out without being asked or requesting compensation. Rural living is a struggle for many. They make ends meet by bartering their skills with the skills of others. We adopted this practice and now barter with friends and colleagues in our network. When we needed several tree stumps to be ground down on our property, rather than hire a commercial vendor, we approached our neighbor who owned and operated a commercial stump grinder. He needed firewood for the winter, of which we had plenty, so he ground our stumps and we provided him with a few face cords of firewood.

All multigenerational living families are in the same boat. We have more to do than hours in the day. As one estate owner said, "Daylight and diesel fuel run out long before I'm ready to be done." It's a new way of living for us. Multigenerational estate visits provide us with many new ideas about activities that we may attempt on our own property. Learning how another family has, for instance, cleared trails, put in bridges, and cut a path through the forest opens up new possibilities about your own property. The best thing about meeting other owners is their willingness to help. With all the activity taking place on your estate, life can get messy and confusing very quickly. Too many people doing too many projects can cause stress and turmoil especially when done at cross purposes or without bad intentions. As always, keep open the lines of communication to lessen any tension.

Multigenerational Living

* * *

The next chapter will dive into the multigenerational living estate operating platform devised to keep everything on track, make it understandable to all, and make it easy to determine who is doing what, when, and why.

22

The Multigenerational Living Estate Operating Platform

During the transaction stage, your family met regularly to ensure the purchase of your estate continued to move along successfully. After moving into your property, as the excitement and stress of the transaction fade, you'll suddenly realize the enormity of the undertaking you've accepted to live together on one property.

During the lead-up to closing on your property, you will have had many discussions and made plans about various changes, updates, fixes, additions, and other matters once closing is completed. Perhaps your move-in date may be in the future after minor or new construction or other changes. No matter the status of your living arrangement, you will have many projects and items to attend to.

The Five-Year Plan

Stepping back for a moment to the first stage, when each family member and your collective family completed your vision/purpose for your estate, is a good place to start. Review your vision. Jumping into a variety of projects before clearly defining the direction your family wants to pursue can waste time, energy, money, and resources. The vision for your property covers your future generations. It is a long-term, multigenerational approach, so what you do now will have a long-term effect.

Living on your estate requires you to take an organized, systemic approach to place rules and boundaries for your family to operate within. Much of this will be derived from the governance established in the first stage. Prioritizing the must-dos, the project list, and the day-to-day activity on your estate is driven by your family vision. That vision needs to be translated into reality, and the farthest out to establish that "reality" is a five-year plan. As part of the Multigenerational Estate Operating Platform (MEOP), everything starts with your five-year plan.

The five-year plan establishes directionality along the same line and in the spirit of your family vision statement. In its simplest form, the five-year plan identifies projects to be completed, events, new opportunities, new capabilities, new businesses, and other initiatives set forth by your leadership team. The leadership team is the group of family members living on the property and following the MEOP.

There will be certain initiatives, such as establishing a new operating business, that will affect non-resident multigenerational living members. The leadership team may include a family member representing the entire family who lives off the estate. Having representation at the five-year planning meeting will ensure all areas of the family vision are included. This off-resident leadership team member will not necessarily be present for periodic multigenerational estate operating meetings or weekly meetings set up through the MEOP.

Your five-year plan is broken into the various initiatives by year, and then a one-year plan is put in place. The leadership team meets for a full day annually to review the results of the past year, reviews the five-year plan, and sets forth the following year's projects and initiatives. This one-year plan addresses everything that will be continued or initiated over the next year. The one-year plan is then broken down roughly into what will be accomplished each quarter. A ninety-day period seems to be the right amount of time to cycle through before life gets more complicated, confusing, and even overwhelming. Your family may or may not have family members other than the leadership team present at the annual planning meeting.

The MEOP has a structure to follow. It starts with establishing all the tasks that will be accomplished over the next quarter. Those tasks are broken down into a 30/60/90 list. The 30/60/90 document is a tool created by Strategic Coach to provide their entrepreneurs with an organized method of completing tasks over the next quarter. It's a tool we have used successfully for the past twenty-five years. Your goal is to accomplish all of the tasks from your 30/60/90. Accomplishing 80 percent of those tasks is completely acceptable. Why only 80 percent? Earlier, we reviewed the learning and winning mindset and the progress, not perfection approach. Life throws a lot at us. Living on your family estate raises the complexity of everything based on the increased inter-relatedness of family members and the multitude of variables around your small town. Aim for progress rather than perfection and living will be smoother.

Many organizations, such as Strategic Coach, Vistage, YPO, and many mastermind groups, meet at least on a quarterly basis. Some of them meet more often. Quarterly meetings tend to work well in the entrepreneurial world for us to recharge, reset, and review the last quarter's results along with the forward planning for the upcoming quarter. Each time new ground is broken, we take two steps forward and one step back. To effectively move forward again, you must simplify to multiply. The MEOP allows for that simplification to again move forward two steps.

Weekly Meetings

The MEOP is structured with a weekly standing meeting lasting no more than an hour to discuss and review several areas. There are four different roles performed by family or non-family members in the MEOP. The first is the CEO or "town mayor," as we affectionately call it. The CEO's role is primarily a leadership role, setting the pace and tempo of the multigenerational living estate by following and living the primary family vision/purpose as stated in the family vision statement. The multigenerational estate operator (MEO) is tasked with all of the operations and functions taking place on the property. The weekly meeting's agenda is prepared and overseen by the MEO. There may be one or more team leaders who head up various parts of the operations on your estate from infrastructure, fields, forest, ponds/streams to business operations or other family operations. They report to the MEO. Finally, there are the team members, those who do the work. These roles, other than the CEO, can be filled by outside staff or family members.

During the weekly meeting, the first action is a review of the past week, along with a review of all tasks for the quarter that have been completed to date. Next, the upcoming schedule for the week, which includes vendor appointments and tasks to be worked on by various parties. Each member at the meeting reviews their open initiatives and reports on the status of the actions being worked on for the quarter. A reminder: Remember to also review the plans for "fun" on your multigenerational living property. More on that later.

Multigenerational living estates may employ permanent staff who maintain the property, work on projects, perform household tasks, and work on multigenerational businesses and other activities. Outside vendors typically view multigenerational living estates as little towns that are treated as commercial customers. It is normal to have at least one outside vendor on the property on a weekly basis. In the first year or two, there may be more vendors than just one weekly. MEOs provide a structure to schedule, coordinate, supervise, and report on progress made by vendors.

During the weekly family meeting, review the coordination of these outside vendors as well as full-time or part-time staff. Estate family members may want to be involved in various parts of the property's operations. Our family has five key leadership team members who oversee the forest, fields, ponds, businesses, and mechanicals on the property. Families will naturally be attracted to and get involved or oversee team members working in their area of interest.

Most entrepreneurs will want to focus solely on their core business, most likely unrelated to multigenerational estate business, and delegate the day-to-day operations to the MEO. The MEO should have a background in the maintenance and upkeep of the buildings and grounds. Typically, an outside party or parties may need to run the day-to-day while the MEO oversees operations.

Multigenerational Living

Requests from family members living on your property will come in daily. Sometimes, functional, mechanical, or other issues need to be addressed immediately. It is not unusual for something to break each week. We have 21,000 square feet of conditioned space in four buildings with over twenty-five thermostats for heat pumps, radiant floor heating, and electric, heating oil, and wood-stove sources of energy. Add in twenty-plus bedrooms, fifteen baths, four septic fields, and four wells. Something will break every week.

Quarterly Meetings

The weekly multigenerational living estate leadership meeting creates order out of chaos. Once each quarter, a 30/60/90 extended meeting is held. The first agenda item is for each leadership team member to review what was accomplished over the past ninety days. Invariably and consistently, about 80 percent of what was planned was accomplished. Remember, living on a multigenerational living estate is about progress not perfection.

Dan Sullivan and Benjamin Hardy wrote *The Gap And The Gain®* in 2021.[11] The synopsis of the book is to always measure results backward. By measuring backward, we can see and focus on what has been accomplished, not on what hasn't been accomplished. There are way too many variables involved in living multi-generationally on an estate. Dan identifies "the gap" as the 20 percent that was not accomplished, and the gain is the 80 percent that has been accomplished. By focusing on "the gain," we maintain a learning and winning mindset. More importantly, you maintain a high level of confidence about where you are and the future of your estate.

The level of learning on a multigenerational living estate is enormous. When there are a dozen family members combined with a dozen structures on over a dozen acres, there's going to be some chaos, frustration, misunderstanding, and confusion, along with feelings of hopelessness, anxiety, and, in some cases, despair. Seriously, maintaining a positive attitude can be extremely difficult unless everyone focuses on what is being accomplished: progress, not perfection.

During the quarterly meeting, you'll briefly review the annual goals and five-year goals. The next quarter's 30/60/90 tasks are then recorded. The leadership team approves the goal to be accomplished in the next quarter and then moves on to the weekly agenda and meeting.

The MEOP allows each family to bring order out of chaos, provide a channel for communication to other multigenerational living members, and be clearly informed on what to address and accomplish next. This provides a consistent level of confidence while getting things accomplished.

Multigenerational living estates can quickly suck a lot of cash out of the operating budget due to the number of projects, repairs, and maintenance and operating expenses. A cash flow accounting and tax structure becomes very important to put in place, monitor, and adjust. Accounting software and financial and tax management are a must-have.

* * *

In Chapter 23, we'll look at finances more deeply and how they will affect your estate, your businesses, philanthropy, and your family.

23

Financials, Business, and Philanthropy

Finances matter deeply, especially when living multi-generationally on your estate. Money touches every area of our life. Most Americans have a variety of dysfunctions around money. It is only in the last two generations that our society has enjoyed building wealth that outlives us, much like the gilded class and "carriage trade" beginning in the early twentieth century. Recognizing this fundamental shift that affects over 10 million Americans has determined how my wealth management company delivers our services. We have developed and delivered our services using a framing formula to simplify how wealth management services are delivered:

$$WoE = IC + RP + DS$$

- WoE stands for the **Wealth of Everything**. Multigenerational living estates are squarely centered on the tangible and intangible aspects of the Wealth of Everything.

- IC stands for **Investment Consulting**. It is the part of wealth management that most people believe is what advisers do on a day-to-day basis. Investment consulting is important because of the role it plays in providing both income and growth for the future. These "investable assets" and other income-producing assets, like real estate, provide the cash flow that ultimately supports estate operations. The other parts of investment consulting are taxes generated by the portfolio and increasing/decreasing levels of assets on the balance sheet.

- RP stands for **Relationship Partnership**. Every family of means typically has accounting, legal, insurance, banking, and extended family member relationships that work with and coordinate with your money and your family. Building a trusted relationship to ensure every party is on your agenda becomes very important when living multi-generationally on your family's estate. The more relationships involved in your life, the more complicated and complex your finances will be.

- The third piece of wealth management, **Deep Support** (DS), is the glue that holds everything together. Deep support is your Easy Button. It provides services no other professional wants to offer or address—all the niggling money and money-related details that happen daily in your life. Deep support involves a lot of "gopher work." The majority of your outside advisers (accountants, attorneys, etc.) tend to be siloed in their approach to providing their services. They provide precisely what they are hired to do and may coordinate some of the parts related to your estate and money. The connections and issues that arise between these various silos can and, many times, cause major issues down the road.

Structuring the Estate's Finances

Multigenerational living estates have many moving parts. Hobbies, businesses, philanthropy, and other initiatives will add to the complexity. We spent over two years structuring the appropriate accounting software to track everything. Sound excessive? It isn't. There are important reasons why sweating out this level of detail matters.

The first and most obvious thing is to understand your basic monthly operating costs. Every cost seems to be magnified on a multigenerational living estate. The multiplication of living space and all the additional or unexpected additional expenses can be stunning.

Estate finances tend to be structured in one of three ways. The most common, based on my research, is covered by the first-generation wealth-building family. Some of these founding families will fund everything. This approach does not work long-term. Not having skin in the game or a sense of the operating expenses, especially as these expenses naturally increase over time, can create an environment of entitlement among supported estate family members and may result in the dreaded "trust-fund baby" mindset.

Another approach is to set up a homeowners operating agreement (HOA) following the governance set forth in the first stage. An LLC (Limited Liability Corporation) may be set up to shield individual families and family members from many financial risks that could lead to bankruptcy. This approach to ownership and paying operating expenses definitely requires detailed accounting, reconciliation, cash flow, and income tax planning.

The third approach is a combination of the first two. I've found it to be the most common form of operational formation. Family members pay monthly lease payments, while fixed and variable expenses are covered by the founding family.

Check Those IRS Schedules

When multigenerational living estates are established on larger tracts of land, they may apply for an agricultural exemption. An appropriate agricultural exemption will reduce the annual real estate taxes owed on the property. This exemption is satisfied by meeting the specific agricultural guidelines of the county or municipality that governs the property. Acceptable agricultural businesses are generally based on a specific amount of livestock, such as chickens, pigs, or sheep, or crops, such as vegetables, fruit, and so on. You'll need to research the local agricultural exemption.

Accounting for all expenses in every category becomes important when businesses operate on a multigenerational living estate. A family farming operation is reported on IRS Schedule F (farming), Schedule C (self-employment), or Schedule E (for other entities, including real estate and related businesses). The multigenerational living estate tax return may now require the filing of several of these new schedules due to the various operations happening simultaneously on the property.

The Tax Reform Act of 1986 segregated income received into three categories: active, passive, and portfolio. Deductions can usually only be taken against income within each category.

- **Portfolio** is fairly straightforward: it reports all interest, dividends, ordinary income, and realized capital gains received annually from all sources.

- **Active income** is any income received in the performance of an activity performed over a minimum threshold of five hundred or more hours.
- **Passive income** is the category under which all other income falls.

Generally, any business other than the primary business of a business owner that is invested in is considered passive income. An example of passive income is running a farm operation primarily overseen or supervised for less than five hundred hours a year. The "passive" approach does not allow for active income self-employment write-offs for depreciation or any expense that exceeds income received from the operations. Establishing a new business can generate a large amount of deductions, but only if the individual taxpayer is actively (over five hundred hours) involved in the operation.

Multigenerational estate family members may not want to be involved in the estate businesses, and as a result, you may have fewer write-offs. The entire accounting and tax area is best reviewed with appropriate accounting and tax counsel. This area can save tens of thousands or even hundreds of thousands in taxes when addressed appropriately.

In Stage Three, we referenced various types of legal ownership. Multigenerational living estates may be owned entirely by the founding family, in an HOA-type ownership arrangement, or a combination thereof. It's important to note whether the estate assets should be considered for transfer to future generations right from the onset of ownership. This is a decision you make with appropriate corporate and estate legal counsel. It may be a smart decision to "remove" the estate from any future exposure to possible transfer (estate) taxes by succeeding generations.

We structured our estate differently than the standard ownership. Our accounting structure tracks and monitors all estate operations: employment, self-employment, farm operations, internal and external leasing, product sales, and other miscellaneous income and expenses. All income and expenses run through the software for a thorough and complete accounting. The accounting firm then runs through all the appropriate schedules to report and deduct all expenses and thereby pays the appropriate federal, state, and municipal taxes.

Charitable Giving

How does philanthropy, in particular, formal philanthropy, come into play in a multigenerational living estate? Surveys conducted over the past several decades consistently report that approximately one-third of all Americans want to consider some kind of formal philanthropy. Formal philanthropy is any individual service or funds for charitable purposes that goes beyond the typical "check-writing" approach to philanthropy. We've all been asked to donate money to help a variety of charitable causes and then write a check with the acknowledgment of thanks for the donation.

Formal philanthropy may involve private non-operating or operating foundations, charitable entities, such as charitable remainder/annuity, charitable lead trusts, or the popular donor-advised fund. Each one of these charitable entities has a different purpose with different levels of involvement. The most involved are private operating or non-operating foundations. Non-operating foundations are less involved and are a great gateway to annually giving to charitable causes most important to a family. Private operating and public operating foundations generally have an operating charitable focus or goal and employ staff for ongoing operational purposes, such as the Red Cross or other popular charities that have an operating purpose to fulfill.

Multigenerational living families will normally stick to the non-operating private foundation or fund a donor-advised fund (DAF). DAFs don't require any involvement and exist to access charitable beneficiaries if and when the donor decides to do so. In the past, we were involved in a support role with a therapeutic horse-riding private charity. This horse farm provides therapy for disabled children. Their operations could easily be operating on a multigenerational living estate as part of the vision and purpose of the family.

* * *

Financials, business, and philanthropy are necessary parts of operating your multigenerational living estate. For many types of businesses, for-profit or not-for-profit, that may be formed on your property, take the time to seek out counsel and understand the depth, resources, time, and money needed to successfully operate these ventures.

Another area requiring your attention is estate security. Security for you and your family is always a number one priority. These family properties have unique characteristics requiring a more customized approach to addressing security. Exploration and understanding of these issues need to be discussed early in the process of occupying your property, and we will explore this topic in the next chapter.

24

Family Security

"**P**eople sleep peaceably in their beds at night only because rough men stand ready to do violence on their behalf."[12] This quote by columnist Richard Grenier, which represents the sentiments of George Orwell, reminds us how our rule of law and governance of that law play out in the United States. We are not as dangerous a place to live as may be implied by the history of recent events. There will always be those who would do violence upon us due to their violent nature and criminal behavior.

Due to your property's larger footprint, your estate and family are more vulnerable to the criminal element, making having security for those living there a priority. When it comes to personal security, you certainly hope for the best but plan for the worst. The presence of multiple families is beneficial to protect each other and to protect against attempts of violence on your property.

An obvious threat is from shipping services like Amazon Prime, UPS, FedEx, and others who have direct access to your property. They come and go at all times

Multigenerational Living

throughout the day and night. You may find them wandering around your roads or walking around various buildings, trying to determine where to drop off packages. They may be well-meaning individuals, or they may be the exception by "casing" your place for an opportunity to commit a robbery or other violence.

Very wealthy families may have private security firms to screen companies and their employees who may commit crimes against their families. One of the shocking statistics I learned from a protective service organization was that over 50 percent of employees of certain catering companies are made up of ex-convicts. The security firm frequently conducts background checks on these catering services prior to the family hiring them for a private event on their property.

It turns out that the highest incidence of identity theft occurs most often when someone gains access to your property. Although not a violent crime per se, identity theft can cause financial harm to family members when a property is not secure from outside parties.

One of the ranch families we interviewed takes security measures very seriously. They are all trained at various levels of self-defense. They believe that America is not as safe a place as it was in the past. Some of them have put together an Everyday Carry (EDC) kit that is with them at all times. Their EDC generally has a pistol, knife, pepper spray, and other items that are easily accessible and ready to use all day, every day.

One of the hard truths to accept is that any family of wealth, depicted by the presence of generous amounts of land, buildings, and infrastructure, is more vulnerable to both non-violent and violent crime. Precautions to protect against any possible crime against your family are prudent and recommended. The level of preparation is an important subject for the multigenerational living council to address.

If your property is fenced, one of the most obvious features is a gate to control access. It is a given that you will have daily deliveries and service calls on your property. The list of possible parties with ready access is fairly extensive: full- or part-time employees, periodic visits by service providers for cleaning, maintenance, landscaping/lawn care, and a variety of trades to conduct infrastructure repair, improvements, and servicing.

Should you operate businesses on your property, you may require a separate entrance to work areas, venues, agricultural, or other land available for business or trade. When business requires heavy daily or seasonal access, you may require a wall or fence around the gated family living area to keep out visitors to your private property.

Consider employing security services to monitor sensitive areas of your multigenerational living estate using security cameras, motion detector devices, and electronic surveillance. As mentioned earlier, some families use services that monitor internet traffic to detect any existential threats to family members. These obviously more serious measures are necessary when family members are well-known business, community, political, entertainment, or sports personalities.

Putting together a security plan, no matter how simple or complex, is a good practice to consider as you take possession of and occupy your multigenerational living estate. You do live in a small town. Situational awareness and knowing what to do in the event of a developing violent situation are imperative. You need to consider what measures you need to take to have your own "police" force.

A "farm" dog may, at first blush, seem to be more pet than protector. Farm dogs take on several roles for your family. They protect vulnerable prey animals (chickens, rabbits, turkeys, etc.) from common predators such as coyotes, foxes, and raccoons. They also serve as your first alert

Multigenerational Living

and defense against anybody coming onto the property to harm family members. They can provide personal protection in close quarters to the more vulnerable members of your family.

With the advent of drone technology and other newer technologies, security measures have stepped up on some multigenerational living estates. Your family estate could put up 24/7 or continuous nighttime drone surveillance of the perimeter and other valuable or sensitive parts of your property. They now have the capacity to detect infrared light and identify threats very quickly, relaying that information to family members internally and to external protection for your property.

You may have other vulnerabilities to consider in setting up your property's security. From protecting sensitive research and development to protecting high-end valuable crops, woodlands, animals, and other specialties. Your little town needs the proper measures in place to protect your oasis of peace and harmony. Be sure to include it in your weekly and quarterly meetings.

* * *

Family security can be a "heavy" subject; it has many parts that we would rather avoid than address. We can't say the same, however, for those family traditions, culture, and newly formed activities that put the "fun" into your multigenerational living estate.

25

Daily and Seasonal Fun and Family Traditions

When I grew up in the 1960s, Sunday was a day of rest. In the summertime, we would picnic at a favorite location, ultimately ending up at Cayuga Lake State Park in upstate New York. We enjoyed boating, water skiing, fishing, and sandbar swimming, plus much more. In the winter, Sunday dinner was at 2:00 PM, and we wore our Sunday "best" clothing all day. Additionally, my parents and grandparents passed down many holiday traditions.

Family traditions have a life and a storied past, and we make memories through many special occasions. Families have a heart and a soul that only members viscerally feel and understand. Whether it's Aunt Susie's famous upside-down pineapple cake or Grandma's pot roast, Grandpa's bad hearing from serving in World War II, or cousin Pete's angelic voice, each family member is known for something they contribute to the family.

Multigenerational Living

Starting on your new phase in living multi-generationally will certainly bring about new traditions and adjustments to family culture, focus, and fun. This may be the first opportunity for family members to pursue interests that were not practical in a suburban or urban environment. Your family members may fulfill their purpose in this brand-new environment. This is unlike the old adage that the grass is greener on the other side. This transition to your forever home may truly be "greener" than your former condition.

While interviewing multigenerational living estate owners, they relayed how they didn't necessarily end up where they anticipated. On two occasions, the children moved back to "the farm" to try out the lifestyle with only them and mom and dad. Fast forward some thirty years, and they are now mom and dad. Related families came and went. In both cases, they now have multiple families occupying multiple homes on their family farm properties. What started as two families has turned into a family farm compound. Not everyone is involved in farming, but they enjoy cohabitating with their close family members.

One family has an event center on the top floor of their home and built another event center, a spacious 160-by-60-foot space for offices, a game room, a multimedia center, and a gathering space that may handle 120 persons. Several multigenerational estate owners have built or modified buildings to house corporate retreats. Others have refitted Airstream trailers or built "tiny houses." There are as many different combinations as there are family properties.

On one hundred-year-old multigenerational living estate, family members meet each summer annually for three weeks. Now in their seventies, twenty-two cousins come together to visit, enjoy each other's company, and enjoy the peace and serenity of their property tucked away in the mountains. Throughout the remainder of the year, two families, representing two of the four branches of the family, live permanently on and watch over the family ranch.

The pace and experience of living a nuclear family way of life are not as conducive to hosting bigger gatherings or events. Several years may pass before your family focuses on new traditions. You may find that a multigenerational living estate can suck you into focusing on the buildings and grounds but not necessarily on camaraderie and fellowship with your fellow family members. There's no doubt that change is the operative word, especially in the first few years. In Chapter 20, we reviewed how it takes two years to know a habit. Allow yourself this time to deepen family relationships, form new bonds, and learn to appreciate other family members. This will bring about a change in how we perceive each other in a brand-new light.

We owned a horse farm in the late 90s in a rural area of Wisconsin. Rural living, rural people, and being surrounded by many dairy farms was a profoundly new experience for us. The local school population was small enough that our children knew everyone in their class. Helping out a neighbor went far beyond borrowing a cup of sugar. The openness to help, to drop everything and assist your neighbors in a crisis is not typically found when you live the suburban or urban lifestyle.

Your multigenerational living estate may be geographically located someplace different enough that many changes will occur over the first few years. Be patient and give yourself time to get accustomed to the changes in lifestyle. Many families immediately add farm animals to the mix. Like dealing with pets, domesticated animals require a lot of your time and attention. Chickens, goats, a cow, and other animals will change your life. You'll need to tend to them seven days a week. Leaving your family estate

Multigenerational Living

overnight will require other family members to step up and pitch in. It may be necessary, in some cases, to barter with neighbors or hire help to handle the animals. Meanwhile, every fox, coyote, hawk, eagle, and other predator will be looking to make a meal out of your smaller prey animals.

Everything and anything can overwhelm you. You must seek out downtime, alone time, fun time! Working your fingers to the bone was not part of your long-term vision or purpose. You didn't envision spending so much time on the buildings, grounds, and businesses. When annually reviewing your one-year plan, make certain to schedule many fun activities and events.

Stop and smell the roses long enough to take in all that your property has to offer you. Nature is soothing. Studies have shown that the fractal (repeating) patterns of nature calm down our amygdala (which regulates our fight-or-flight response) and our inner critic. You know, that voice that says you can't do this or that, you are not worthy, you tried that before and failed, and other negative self-talk.

One of the second-generation owners of a longtime established family ranch stated, "One of my favorite sports on the ranch is to do absolutely nothing. I almost always get a lot accomplished." He's right; we can accomplish so much in silent contemplation, relaxation, and tranquility while the whole world goes by. Our soul and our mind need time to coalesce, think, and still.

One of my early mentors said, "Gary, you need to slow down to speed up." We can run ourselves ragged on the hamster wheel of life. Taking the time to think slowly and then act is one of the greatest lessons I've learned about life. Living on your multigenerational living estate is set up exactly for that. The open spaces allow for "non-time," as author Steven Kotler (a Flow expert) stated.[13] Non-time is planned time to simply relax and take in whatever floats to the surface of your being.

Fun on your property has so many parts. You'll enjoy time with family members, appreciate time alone in a quiet living space or corner of the property, and savor new family traditions that are only practiced on a multigenerational living estate. No matter how you find your fun, it will mean so much more because you're sharing this new life with your extended family.

Conclusion

Your journey of transforming your family from single-family households to multi-generational living is definitely a worthwhile journey. There are chapters in this book that may dissuade you from seeing your vision to that future and completion. Many years ago, one of my mentors stressed to me that all progress starts by telling yourself the truth. I did not hold back on that truth here.

Starting where you need to start is very important. Establishing trust and communication will see your family through difficult discussions. Understanding how to resolve a seemingly irreparable impasse through conflict resolution results in burning no bridges.

Your family vision is always the touchstone, the centerpiece, the essence, and the heart of who you are and why you chose this seemingly unusual lifestyle, at least as measured by societal norms.

Rules. We need them because they keep everything in balance. Guardrails on a bowling alley are there, no matter if you roll a gutter ball or a strike. There is another play happening again and again because the ball is returned for another play in life while still living on the bowling alley of your estate.

Many years ago, I was "forced" to watch a flower arrangement being designed because I sat in the front row. The young woman started with, "Building a flower arrangement is all about the proper structure." My ears perked up. I understand structure! "First put in the green spongy square in the center of the vase. Then, push in a flower every 90 degrees around the spongy green thingy. Then repeat." Wow! I can make a flower arrangement. Who knew?

Seriously, structure does that for us. It brings clarity out of chaos. Intentionally making decisions by the process of elimination greases the wheels of change, allowing the process to move forward more smoothly. Being clear about your negotiables and non-negotiables on the what, how, and why of your property limits your choices in a good way.

Operating under the spirit of your guiding principles keeps your family headed in the same direction. Applying the "arrangement" of your personal and family finances, taxes, and risk, along with intentionally addressing your estate, keeps the monies structured to support your current living and future growth. These two very important stages of foundational development and structure allow you to have as smooth of a transaction as possible in the purchase of your property. Constant communication, along with reminding each person of the reason for putting yourself through this difficult process, allows for the transaction to come to completion.

Joy. Fun. Excitement. Enthusiasm. Peace. All of these emotional states of mind begin to play out as you live on your family estate. This is truly a transformational experience. You are now living your dream of re-engaging, reconnecting, and renewing the most important parts of who you and your family represent. This is a journey with

Multigenerational Living

its ebbs and flows. Birth, death, separation, health, and all the other trials and tribulations are now shared and supported by your family members. This is truly living the way you have always intended to live.

I hope this book eases your transition into multi-generational living. One day, we may meet either on your estate or mine. You will share your experiences, which, yet again, we'll learn from and bring back to my family. My hope for you and your family is that you will fulfill your deepest purpose, vision, and desires to pass along to the next generations and that those next generations will have greater wisdom than we possess, living out their intentional, purposeful lives for the betterment of their family, their community, and the world at large.

Endnotes

[1] Robin Dunbar, "Neocortex Size as a Constraint on Group Size in Primates," *Journal of Human Evolution* 22, no. 6 (June 1992): 469–93, https://doi.org/10.1016/0047-2484(92)90081-j.

[2] Roy O. Williams and Vic Preisser, *Preparing Heirs: Five Steps to a Successful Transition of Family Wealth and Values* (Bandon, OR: Robert D. Reed Publishers, 2014).

[3] John Hunter, "Before Deming's 14 Points for Management," The W. Edwards Deming Institute, September 29, 2015, https://deming.org/before-demings-14-points-for-management/.

[4] "What Is Active Listening?," United States Institute of Peace, November 24, 2021, https://www.usip.org/public-education-new/what-active-listening#:~:text=Active%20listening%20is%20a%20way,is%20important%20in%20managing%20conflicts.

[5] "Are You an Informed or Uninformed Taxpayer?," Biblical Stewardship Resource Library, accessed March 25, 2024, https://stewardshiplibrary.com/are-you-an-informed-or-uninformed-taxpayer/.

[6] Dan Sullivan, "The 4 Freedoms That Motivate Successful Entrepreneurs," Strategic Coach, accessed April 4, 2024, https://resources.strategiccoach.com/the-multiplier-mindset-blog/the-4-freedoms-that-motivate-successful-entrepreneurs.

7. Sheena Iyengar, *The Art of Choosing* (New York, NY: Twelve, 2022).
8. Peter H. Diamandis and Steven Kotler, *Bold: How to Go Big, Create Wealth and Impact the World* (London: Simon & Schuster, 2017).
9. Daniel Kahneman, *Thinking Fast and Slow* (New York, NY: Farrar, Straus and Giroux, 2011).
10. "1. A Cup of Tea," Zen Koans, accessed March 28, 2024, https://ashidakim.com/zenkoans/1acupoftea.html.
11. Dan Sullivan and Benjamin Hardy, *The Gap And The Gain: The High Achievers Guide to Happiness, Confidence, and Success* (Carlsbad, CA: Hay House, Inc., 2021).
12. Richard Grenier, "Perils of Passive Sex," *The Washington Times*, April 6, 1993.
13. Steven Kotler, "3 Science-Based Strategies to Increase Your Creativity ," ideas.ted.com, January 29, 2021, https://ideas.ted.com/3-science-based-strategies-to-increase-your-creativity/.

Acknowledgments

I wouldn't have been inspired to write this book without the seven generations of over 110 souls who impacted me, my mindset, and my thinking. I was blessed to have special relationships with so many of them: Great-grandfather Miller taught me and three of my sisters how to play the card game Pinochle. Great-grandmother Miller spent several Easter weeks with us. I remember snowmobiling and exploring with Grandma and Grandpa DeRocha and learning to bowl from Grandpa Vincentini. There were many (eavesdropped) conversations between my mother and Grandma Vincentini that reinforced the importance of a family bond. I always looked forward to fishing, watching TV, and Sunday suppers with my Grandfather and Grandmother Klaben. My parents showed me the importance of hard work as they dedicated themselves to raising me and my nine siblings. Our foundation of faith, family, and service led to many opportunities in my life. My wonderful, talented, and supportive siblings were with me through so many life experiences that formed my love for family and the many facets through the many generations.

I would be a much different, much lesser person without my wife, Debra. My children, Sarah and John, thank you for teaching me so much about how to be a better person and a better father. To their wonderful spouses, Andrew and Joy, thank you for your support in helping raise our wonderful grandchildren, Ethan, Sullivan, and GiGi.

To the other families on our family estate: Bob and Sandy, Diane and Gamal, Jennifer and Doug (Casey, Matt, Seth, and Catalina), thank you for taking my lead in joining us on this new journey of growth and discovery. I would be remiss to exclude our other future generations of family members: our 32 nieces and nephews and 34 great nieces and nephews, along with their spouses and our great-grandniece.

Our company team, especially Kevin Coyle, has unwaveringly supported me for more than four decades on everything imaginable. Dave Smestuen, thank you for supporting this book and its undertaking. Thank you, Katie Hickman, for the many hours of advice, editing, and fieldwork to complete this book. Aleks and Rachelle have provided me with the time to write and so many other creative endeavors. I appreciate the dedicated team at Inspiring Souls who have dedicated their purpose to the entrepreneurial business book writer. To the 20 families who graciously agreed to be interviewed about their family estates, your stories and insights were invaluable. To Dan Sullivan and Joe Polish and all the entrepreneurs they have connected me to over the past three decades, thank you.

Finally, to you, who are about to embark on this brave new adventure to form your multigenerational family estate, I hope the wisdom I've shared makes your journey to multigenerational living a success.

About the Author

Gary Klaben is the Principal of Coyle Financial, a wealth management firm near Chicago. He has over 30 years of experience and specializes in high-touch holistic financial services for business owners and high-net-worth families. As a published author, Gary has written transformative books such as *Changing the Conversation: Transformational Steps to Financial and Family Well-Being*, *Wealth of Everything*, and *The Business Battlefield* (co-authored with Adam Blonsky).

In addition to his writing, Gary is a seasoned speaker and serves as a coach and mentor for entrepreneurs. He is a West Point graduate and a former infantry officer and holds the designations Chartered Financial Consultant (ChFC) and Chartered Life Underwriter (CLU) and has a Master of Science in Financial Services (MSFS). Gary's military background is marked by graduating as the top student in his Ranger School class after attending West Point, shaping his unwavering dedication to service.

Gary resides in a multigenerational family estate in Reisterstown, MD, embodying a well-rounded approach to life.

CONNECT WITH GARY

Follow him on LinkedIn today

MultiGenBook.com

GARY IS HERE TO HELP!

Build a multi-generational family legacy that goes beyond finances.

MultiGenBook.com

Book Gary for Keynote Speaking

Start the conversation today!

MultiGenBook.com

THIS BOOK IS PROTECTED INTELLECTUAL PROPERTY

EASY IP®

The author of this book values Intellectual Property. The book you just read is protected by Easy IP®, a proprietary process, which integrates blockchain technology giving Intellectual Property "Global Protection." By creating a "Time-Stamped" smart contract that can never be tampered with or changed, we establish "First Use" that tracks back to the author.

Easy IP® functions much like a Pre-Patent™ since it provides an immutable "First Use" of the Intellectual Property. This is achieved through our proprietary process of leveraging blockchain technology and smart contracts. As a result, proving "First Use" is simple through a global and verifiable smart contract. By protecting intellectual property with blockchain technology and smart contracts, we establish a "First to File" event.

Protected By Easy IP®

LEARN MORE AT EASYIP.TODAY

Printed in Great Britain
by Amazon